Career Crossroads:
Finding the Perfect Career for This Time in Your Life

This book is a work of non-fiction. Unless otherwise noted, the authors and the publisher make no explicit guarantee as to the accuracy of the information contained in this book. In some cases, names of people and places have been changed to protect their privacy.

Career Crossroads: Finding the Perfect Career for This Time in Your Life

First published by Jumping Duck Media

ISBN-10: 0-9820242-0-7
ISBN-13: 978-0-9820242-0-1

Printed in the United States of America

JUMPING DUCK MEDIA

This book is dedicated to Cleon Cox III, who passionately
teaches us to "have fun, learn something, and meet new people."

contents

FORWARD

The job search process can be a challenge, even under the best of circumstances. These days, the internet has made it easy for job seekers to mass-distribute their profile online. However, it has also increased the clutter for hiring managers and recruiters, making it much more difficult for good candidates to rise to the top of the stack.

When it comes to finding the perfect career, you can no longer simply send out resumes and wait for the phone to ring. In today's environment, it is important to have a more refined plan for success in the job search. The four steps of the Career Crossroads ARMS process, as outlined in this book, give job seekers a methodology for successfully cutting through the clutter to help them find the perfect career.

Though written as a stand-alone resource, this book is a component of the CMS Career Crossroads system, available at **cmscareerxroads.com**. Online resources include videos, worksheets, and online coaching. Also, there are social networking groups, blogs, and forums available for clients to assist each other in the career marketing process. Some of these resources are free to all. Others require a nominal fee. In addition to this, seminars, workshops and one-on-one coaching are all available through CMS. Feel free to visit us online to find out more.

We hope that you will utilize these resources to find the perfect career fit for this time in your life, and that you will have fun in the process. This can be a rich and fulfilling time of growth! Use the tools here to enhance your job search and to enrich your life.

thank you

We are grateful to so many people for assisting in this project! We hope we haven't left anyone out! Gary Prehn, Rodger Cook, Eric Mann, Tim Clark, Pete Wright, Janeice Gray, Nancy Besson, Bob Keyser, Ben Rowe, Frank Bender, Megan Strand, Dick and Evelyn Harry, Brandi Kajino, Noah Brockman, Chris Seymour, Jim Nudelman, Christina Caponi, Phill Yoon, Sabine Welling, Arrada Mahamitra, Michael Thompson, Jeff Lampson, Jeff Millard, Courtney LeBoeuf, Mel Myers and Kathie Nelson. Three companies have also played major rolls in the creation of all these materials: The Park Avenue Café, SOUK, and Fifth and Main. Thank you all for teaching, inspiring and encouraging us throughout this endeavor!

Job search effectiveness curve

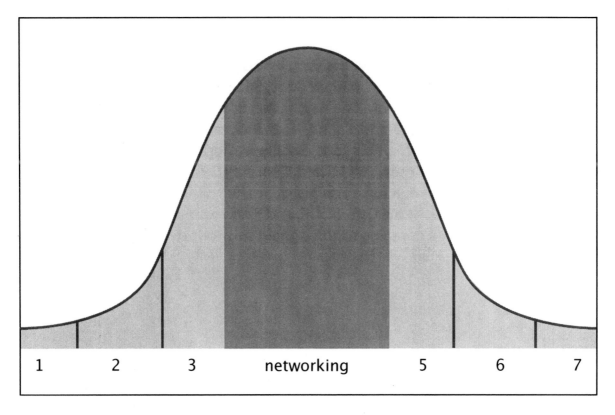

1) All online resume postings combined
2) Newspaper
3) Recruiter
   Networking
5) Government
6) Company website
7) "Out of the blue"

Introduction

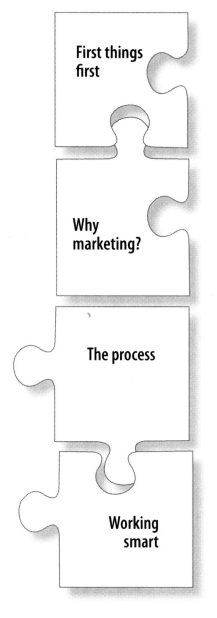

First things first

Why marketing?

The process

Working smart

FIRST THINGS FIRST

If you're reading this, you want to get more out of your career. Or you're one of the authors' moms. Let's assume we're not related and consider where people usually go wrong when they are in your shoes.

Generally, when people start gearing up to transition positions, they do a few things, like create or fatten up a resume, post it online, and mail it out to every want-ads lead they can get their hands on. Does it work? Not usually. Are they foolish? Not necessarily. That's how things used to get done. But the world of work has evolved.

The bell curve opposite depicts the effectiveness of various methods used to find a job in today's market. On one end of the curve is the combined effectiveness of using internet job boards such as Monster, Jobdango, or Careerbuilder to conduct your search. Roughly two to three percent of job seekers find their job using internet job boards—that's all of the job boards combined! On the other end of the curve, you will note, you have roughly the same chance of finding a job "out of the blue". That means someone comes up to you and offers you a job that you have not been looking for. Roughly one percent of the professional workforce finds their job this way. It actually does happen! That being said, we do not recommend that you rely solely on either technique for your job search. If you do, you can expect it to take a very long time.

By way of contrast, the highest point of the curve represents networking as the most effective means for finding the perfect career position. Recent studies indicate that roughly forty percent of professionals landed their job thanks to some sort of networking activity.

Think about a restaurant. Restaurants have menus, right? Whether they are fancy with pretty fonts, xeroxed copies or chalked up on a board, a menu is a description of what the place offers. That's what a resume does for you. But have you ever chosen a restaurant because of a menu itself? More likely you went because you were in the mood for Thai, or because one of your friends told you what a great place it is. The same holds true for the folks with the keys to the company castle. They are more likely to hire you because they are "in the mood for" someone with your unique abilities, or because you've come to them through someone whose opinion they value. When it comes to getting hired, it's not just about the resume, any more than a restaurant is just about the menu. It's what comes to the table that matters, and that depends on the chef, the ingredients, the vision of the owner. The menu is only a piece of paper that describes what's offered. An important part of the process, indeed, but not the only link in the chain. Similarly, rather than expecting to land a job with a resume, you should think of it as a step in the process. A step, in fact, that comes pretty far down the line from where you are now.

The journey you are undertaking will be based on a four-part process, consisting of Assessment, Research, Marketing Materials and Strategy. Developed by Dr. Sean Harry, we call the system the Harry ARMS treatment. Now that you've got that image stuck in your brain, let's get a little deeper into the details of what it is, how it works, and why.

First of all, this system is not just some new self-help hype. It's based on a process that has been used by career counselors for decades to help upper-level management and CEOs transition from position to position. The difference is that those managers and CEOs typically pay thousands of dollars to have a personal coach walk them through the same steps we provide for you here and online at **cmscareerxroads.com**. The success of the system has been proven throughout the strata of the world of work. It has been included in the curriculum of Portland State University for its Masters in International Management program. Dr. Harry teaches the system there, and at large in the Portland, Oregon community. He has seen hundreds of people find work they love based on its principles.

The ARMS Process

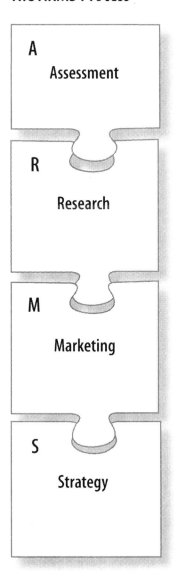

The system, as a whole, is designed to do two things: help you understand why you need a marketing campaign to achieve your career goals, and provide you with a strategy for conducting your career marketing campaign.

WHY MARKETING?

Marketing gurus describe marketing as "the business of renting out space in the mind of the consumer." In the restaurant example used earlier, your friend's recommendation rents out space in your mind, makes it memorable to you, and makes you want to try it for yourself. That's because your friend is a member of your network of friends, and we rely on our networks for trusted information. Therefore, networking is another key component of the ARMS process.

It may be that words like "marketing" and "networking" make you think of glad-handing salesmen pushing their agenda, and you squirm at the idea of becoming one of them. Don't let the possible connotations of the words deprive you of their value. Marketing is nothing more or less than putting your best foot forward. You brush your teeth and wear clean clothes on a date, right? That's marketing. You value the opinions of your friends, and help them out when you can, don't you? That's networking. The very principles that turn date one into dates two and three, or that get you out to this restaurant instead of that one, will be used here to help you get the job you want.

The Four P's of Marketing

Marketers also talk about the Four P's of marketing. They are Product, Price, Place and Promotion. In market-speak, these are factors that can be adjusted based on the marketing environment. The goal of using them is to make strategic decisions that will help enhance a product's value for a target market, resulting in more sales. The ARMS process provides a practical application of these same principles for job seekers. The product is you, the price is the salary and benefits you command, and the place is the industry, company and career position where you work. In this case, positioning deals with the way you present yourself to your target market—a potential employer. The result, or sale, is you in the perfect career position for this time in your life.

Respect Yourself

Another term from the marketing world that you will come to employ is Unique Selling Proposition, or USP. Your USP is what makes you different from everyone else who does the job you do. By way of example, one of Career Crossroads' clients is a chiropractor. They are a dime a dozen in any major metropolitan area. To set himself apart, this chiropractor defines his specialty as working with women who are thirty-nine years old and want to run a marathon on their fortieth birthday. Another client, a Project Manager, was asked to define himself in terms of his career. After several minutes of throwing around terms and figures that sounded like quotes from the Project Manager's 101 Workbook, we asked what he really liked about being a project manager. He paused, thought, and eventually said with a smile, "I like to work with the most difficult people." What organization wouldn't benefit from having someone like that around? Using the Career Crossroads process, you will also learn to define yourself in a way that sets you apart from the crowd.

Consider first not what you want to do, but who you are.

THE PROCESS

One of the biggest stumbling blocks that people encounter in reaching their goals is that they can't define them. No wonder they are frustrated! Therefore, the first step of the ARMS process, Assessment, is designed to help you get a clearer picture of what works for you, so that you can translate that into the work you want to do. Conventional thinking advocates trying to make yourself and your resume match a posted job description. Sadly, that road leads to where you are now, looking for work. How can you feel good about a position that doesn't suit you? We believe that you are better off to define your own knowledge, skills, and abilities, and then find a place where those attributes are in demand. In other words, once you know you are an apple, rather than trying to sell yourself as an orange, you should find out who's in the market for apples in the first place. That's where Research comes in. Online, at the library, and in conversation with professionals in the field, you will find out all about the "apple market", so that you can find out where you best fit into it. In step three, Marketing Materials, you will develop your resources, of which a resume is a part, so that you will be able to make your apple shine. Finally, in Strategy, you are ready to take all you have learned out into the job market. Since most people begin at this stage, distributing resumes, you will stand out among them, thanks to the depth of your knowledge and preparation.

WORKING SMART

Another failure of the "mail out a resume and hope someone calls" procedure is that the only benchmark of progress you have is whether or not you have a job. Using the ARMS process, you have a framework within which to set Specific, Measurable, Attainable, Realistic, and Timely goals. This concept of SMART goal-setting has also been around awhile, and has been proven to work. In each chapter of this text, you will first take an in-depth look at the substance and reasoning of each step of the ARMS process. At the end of the chapter, you will find assignments to complete, and methods for recording and tracking your results. Thus you will have clear benchmarks for measuring your progress throughout the process.

SUMMARY

Hopefully, by now you can see that the Career Crossroads process is rooted in common sense. Begin at the beginning, with yourself, rather than near the end, with your resume. Determine what you want, then find out who wants you. Be prepared to demonstrate your abilities. Connect with the people in field you want to work in. It's not magic. It works.

And so will you.

01Assessment

Assess your personality

Gather feedback

Quantify your abilities

Analyze the data

"Would you tell me, please, which way I ought to go from here?" said Alice to the Cheshire Cat.
"That depends a good deal on where you want to get to," said the Cat.
"I don't much care where..." said Alice.
"Then it doesn't matter which way you go," said the Cat.
Lewis Caroll-Alice's Adventures in Wonderland

What about you?

It's hard to get where you want to go when you don't know what you want. Many job seekers are compelled to make changes due to dissatisfaction with their current work situation, but aren't sure what would make them happier. There's a need, then, to review aspects of both your work and personal life that have brought you the greatest sense of accomplishment and success. These things can help you determine what kind of work would be most rewarding for you.

Assessment is the first step of the ARMS process. In this chapter, you will focus on assessing your abilities. This step will help you determine the things that you do best, that you enjoy the most, and translate these skills into quantifiable factors that will be both descriptive of your abilities and attractive to employers. Achieving an optimal balance between your abilities and the needs of the marketplace produces the highest likelihood of successfully meeting or exceeding job requirements. When you are performing work that you are good at and enjoy doing, you will have a deeper sense of job satisfaction, which lends itself to life satisfaction and an improved sense of self-worth.

The Assessment procedure is made up of four parts. First, you will assess your personality using online resources. Second, you will gather feedback from people you know who can give you their insights into who you are and what careers might be best suited to you. Third, you will review your past achievements and translate them into objective statements regarding your abilities. Finally, you will analyze the data you've gathered to begin developing a picture of your next career position.

ASSESS YOUR PERSONALITY

There are a variety of personality, interest, and career inventories on the market that will assist you in the process of understanding yourself, and based on that understanding, to make career choices that would be most productive for you. They will also help you better understand how you relate to the required tasks of a specific job. Insights into your personality type and how it affects your interactions with family, friends, and others can help you in your life outside work as well.

When you complete the personality preference assessment online, your results will be provided along with a narrative to help you understand it. These results will help you define the characteristics of your personality type, recognize your skills and why you feel a greater sense of accomplishment in completing some tasks than others, and give you insight into the personalities of other people you will encounter as you conduct your career marketing campaign.

We recommend that you take a pragmatic approach to the interpretation of these results. You should take what is helpful and leave the rest. Since we are not using these assessments for therapy, their usefulness is most pronounced in understanding your own hard-wired circuitry.

The following assessment systems are recommended:

- The Keirsey Temperament Sorter
  www.keirsey.com

- The Myers-Brigg Type Indicator
  www.myersbriggs.org

- Strengths Finder 2.0
  www.sf2.strengthsfinder.com

- The Holland Assessment
  www.self-directed-search.com

GATHER FEEDBACK

Many clients gain insights from people with whom they have a personal relationship, or have worked with in the past. These people can often provide valuable knowledge about strengths that clients may fail to recognize within themselves. They can also provide information about "blind spots" that the client may not be aware of.

Send a letter or email to ten to twelve of your friends and colleagues to ask them for input on your professional strengths and weaknesses, as well as to gain their opinions about the type of position that they think would best suit you.

Personal consultation with a CMS Career Crossroads Coach is available to help you get a deeper understanding of how your personality tests can help you most in your career search. Visit **cmscareerxroads.com** to find out more.

QUANTIFY YOUR ABILITIES

Your next step is to complete a Career Accomplishment Self Inventory, or CASI. The goal of this exercise is to provide quantifiable evidence of your past achievements. By studying your past accomplishments you will be better able to market yourself as the product. A thorough and objective understanding of your skills and achievements is vital to developing a clearer picture of the perfect career position for this time of your life.

This activity is our "secret sauce"—everything in your career marketing plan, from here to completion, is based on the work you do in this section. Please take time to complete this as thoroughly as possible! The effort spent here will pay off many times over by the time you have successfully completed your marketing campaign. Remember, owning a fitness manual won't do much make you look sexy at the beach. You have to put in the time and effort to follow its methods. The same is true here.

The CASI is a five-step process. The first four steps are designed to help you identify your past successes and turn them into measurable results, indicating what career might be best suited to you. In the fifth step you will develop this information into key accomplishment narratives that will be invaluable in developing not only your resume, but in allowing you to express your successes and abilities clearly in interviews. You will find corresponding worksheets to help you through the process in the "assignments" section, at the end of this chapter, as well as being available for you to download at **cmscareerxroads.com**.

CASI
Career **A**ccomplishment **S**elf-**I**nventory

1 List past achievements

2 Transfer data to CASI matrix

3 Identify top achievements

4 Prioritize results

5 Develop narratives

CASI Step One:
List past achievements

Begin by listing a minimum of twenty past accomplishments and successes. To do this, pick a time in your past, whether it be on the job, doing volunteer work, or in some personal pursuit, when you felt you were successful. What was your role in that success? What did you do? What happened as a result?

It will be much easier to analyze your data if you focus on a small part of one of your accomplishments. For example, "Led a team that developed an ad campaign for Wonderful Widgets in the summer of 2005", will be more useful in completing this step than "served as ad campaign leader." Likewise, "sold $426,000 worth of Widge-o-Matics in April 2006" is better than "three-time sales leader." In these examples, the action words "led a team", "developed an ad" and "sold" will be key to completing subsequent steps of the CASI process, so be sure and use words that clearly describe your participation. Also, specific details of time, revenue earned, or money saved will be particularly useful for objectifying your achievements.

Obviously, some accomplishments are easier to quantify than others. Persons who are engaged in sales, finance, and manufacturing can usually point to specific, measurable results, as in the examples above. On the other hand, those involved in leadership, teaching, training and counseling may have a more difficult time quantifying results. For those who work more directly with people, keep in mind accomplishments you have had in regards to saving money, increasing efficiencies, or assisting clients to succeed. How many people were involved? How many events did you plan or lead? How much money did you save the organization by doing this instead of something else?

Focus on a specific part of each accomplishment

Be specific about details of time, money and results

CASI Step Two:
Transfer data to the CASI Matrix

You will now translate the language used in CASI Step One into marks on the CASI Matrix. Each accomplishment from step one relates a number across the top of the Matrix. In other words, your first accomplishment will be represented by column one on the matrix. Each accomplishment will have its own column so you can focus on each one separately. It is important that you focus on one accomplishment at a time in order to get clean data. With that accomplishment in mind, follow the column down the page, and place a check mark in the box, if you feel that accomplishment corresponds with the activity key word listed in that box. Leave the box blank if you feel it does not.

For example, let's look back at step one's "Led a team that developed an ad campaign for Wonderful Widgets in the summer of 2005". Going down the first column of the matrix you will put a check mark in the boxes "Administered," "Advertised," "Advised," "Briefed," "Conceptualized," and so on. "Accounting," "Analyzed," "Artistic," "Assembled," "Audited" and so forth are left blank. Don't get hung up on the "correct definition" for the activity key word. Your first hunch is good enough here. You will refine this list as you go along. Your objective is to gather data by connecting your accomplishments to specific key words. Do not rush this step. In fact, we recommend you complete two accomplishment columns, and then go make a sandwich. Come back and complete two more columns, and then go eat the sandwich. The key here is to keep each accomplishment as narrowly focused as possible so you can get clean data.

Once you have completed the entire list, you will tally up the results. Simply count the number of check marks for each key word and record that number in the total column. At this point you will see that several key words are floating to the top of your list of what you are capable of and willing to do. The next steps will help you narrow that list to a workable handful that will become your key accomplishment narratives.

Value
activities that you enjoy. They indicate work you will enjoy!

CASI Step Three:
Identify top achievements

In this step, your goal is to develop two lists. First, make a top-ten list of categories with the most "hits", or boxes marked. This is a record of you quantitative achievements, and showcases the skills and abilities that you have the most experience with. Second, list your favorite five categories, even if they only have one "hit". This list represents your "qualitative" achievements, and shows the things that you enjoy doing the most. Don't undervalue the activities you enjoy doing, as these are good indicators of what kind of work you will find the most rewarding.

CASI Step Four:
Prioritize results

Carefully review the list from step three. It is now time to begin focusing your knowledge, skills, and abilities down to a workable list. Pay special attention to items that appear on both lists. Choose the top three to four items on the lists that you are both capable of and willing to do in your next career position. These will be your top career accomplishments.

In ranking your successes, remember that you don't have to make a career out of things that you are capable of, but don't want to do. If you hate sorting widgets, you probably shouldn't pursue that as a career, even if you are really good at it. Don't forget, if you know you're an apple, why try and pass yourself off as an orange?

Accept yourself
If you know you are an apple, don't try and sell yourself as an orange!

CASI Step Five:
Develop narratives

Once you have come up with a list of accomplishments that you can and want to use in your new position, you will develop a brief narrative of two to three sentences for each achievement. Describe what you did, for whom, and the measurable results that came about because of your activity. These will be known as your key accomplishment narratives, and you will use them again and again throughout this book.

Once you have completed a brief narrative for each accomplishment, you will complete a second and then a third for the same factors. The rationale behind this is that nearly anyone can come up with one example of their success. Candidates who can give a minimum of three examples of each will set themselves apart from the competition!

These brief narratives will be used to develop your resumes, in your verbal marketing materials, and in interviews. It is important that you spend quality time in preparing your answers for this section.

Key accomplishment narratives are concise descriptions of your top accomplishments

ANALYZE THE DATA

Congratulations! You now have a significant amount of data, gathered from a variety of resources. You can begin to build a description of the type of work that would be most satisfying, and that you are most capable of and willing to do. This description of your knowledge, skills, and abilities should include your experience and indicate where your abilities would be most highly valued.

Do not be concerned about placing a job title on your next career position at this time. The next chapter will help you discover where in the world of work your skills and abilities are most needed.

ASSESSMENT SUMMARY

In any successful marketing plan, the first step is to clearly define the product before identifying the best target market. In career marketing, you are starting with a product that is largely defined by your personal preferences, knowledge, skills, abilities, and experiences.

The investment you have made in this part of the ARMS process is extremely useful for making your current career transition. Understanding your personality type preferences, knowing what others think you should be doing, and clearly stating your successes will become the foundation of your career marketing plan. Once you have a clear picture of who you are and what you have to offer, you can more effectively begin to research the job market, looking for the perfect career position fit.

FUTURE USES

The assessment procedure you have just completed will apply any time you want to transition from one career to the next. You can also use this to substantiate your contributions when you feel you are ready for a raise or a promotion. Being able to clearly state your worth is key in establishing your value to your potential or current employer. You may want to go through this same process regularly, so you will be prepared with the facts whenever new opportunities presents themselves.

Assessment: assignr

Record personality assessment results

Which personality assessment or assessments did you use?

_____

_____

_____

Write a brief description of the opportunities
available to you based on what you learned from your personality profile.

_____

_____

_____

_____

_____

_____

_____

_____

_____

_____

_____

_____

_____

Assessment: assignment two

Send out letters or emails of request for feedback

(see following page for example letter)

Consider the responses

According to the insights provided by friends,
relatives, and co-workers, what are your major professional strengths?

_____

_____

_____

_____

Are there any weaknesses or "blind spots" that were pointed out to you?

_____

_____

_____

_____

What insights have you gained from this information?

_____

_____

_____

_____

Timothy Bryan
2227 Townsend Way
Hollywood, FL 33020
January 19, 2008

Mr. Corbett Bise, Director
Gidgets Widgets
2625 Amistad Drive
Port St. Joe, FL 32456

Dear Mr. Bise,

I have recently engaged Career Management Solutions to assist me
in my preparations for a new career. CMS uses an approach designed
to focus on past achievements and successes. Part of their process is
to determine the strengths, abilities and motivations of their clients.
They want to see their clients as their friends see them, both the good
and not so good.

Will you please write a letter in which you identify what you believe
to be my strong points and my weak points, as well as what you think
I need to be both successful and happy in a career. Please send your
response to me at the above address at your earliest convenience.

Thank you for your time,

Timothy Bryan

Assessment: Assignment three
Career Achievement Self Inventory

CASI step one:
List past achievements

Make a list of twenty things you have accomplished in your work, volunteer, or personal life. Order is not important, but remember to use "action words", and to be specific.

1 _____

_____

2 _____

_____

3 _____

_____

4 _____

_____

5 _____

_____

6 _____

_____

7 _____

_____

8 _____

_____

9 _____

_____

continued next page

10 _____

_____

11 _____

_____

12 _____

_____

13 _____

_____

14 _____

_____

15 _____

_____

16 _____

_____

17 _____

_____

18 _____

_____

19 _____

_____

20 _____

_____

CASI step two:
Transfer the data to the CASI matrix

	1	2	3	4	5	6	7	8	9	10	11	12	13	14	15	16	17	18	19	20
accounting																				
administered																				
advertised																				
advised																				
analyzed																				
artistic																				
assembled																				
audited																				
briefed																				
budgeted																				
conceptualized																				
construction trades																				
controlled the event																				
coordinated																				
counseled individuals or groups																				
created contracts																				
created ideas																				
customer relations																				

continued next page

	1	2	3	4	5	6	7	8	9	10	11	12	13	14	15	16	17	18	19	20
data processing																				
designed																				
developed procedures/processes																				
developed questions																				
diagnosed																				
economized/saved																				
edited																				
electrical																				
enforced rules/procedures																				
established policy/procedures																				
established systems																				
evaluated																				
figured/calculated																				
financial planning/monitoring																				
fixed something																				
grant writing																				
initiated action																				
instructed/trained																				
interviewed																				
inventoried																				
led people																				

	1	2	3	4	5	6	7	8	9	10	11	12	13	14	15	16	17	18	19	20
manged people/things																				
marketing																				
mechanical drawing																				
modified																				
monitored																				
motivated																				
negotiated																				
observed																				
operated																				
organized people																				
organized projects																				
perceived idea																				
persuaded																				
planned																				
problem solving																				
produced item																				
program development																				
programmed computer																				
promoted																				
promoted program																				
public relations																				

continued next page

	1	2	3	4	5	6	7	8	9	10	11	12	13	14	15	16	17	18	19	20
purchased																				
repair work																				
researched																				
resolved problem																				
scheduled																				
seminar or workshop speaker																				
sold/marketed																				
spoke in public																				
supervised																				
taught/lectured																				
tended																				
time management																				
troubleshooting																				
wrote reports																				
wrote/published																				

CASI step three:
Identify top factors

Now make two lists. The first is a list of your top ten hits. To do this, record the ten categories from the matrix that got the greatest number of marks. For the second list, record the five categories that are your favorites—things you really enjoy— even if they only got one mark. You will later use these combined fifteen factors to describe your next career position.

Top ten hits:

1 _____

2 _____

3 _____

4 _____

5 _____

6 _____

7 _____

8 _____

9 _____

10 _____

Five favorites:

1 _____

2 _____

3 _____

4 _____

5 _____

CASI step four:
Prioritize results

From the two lists on the preceeding page, list three to five career abilities that you are both capable of and willing to use.

_____

_____

_____

_____

_____

_____

_____

_____

CASI step five:
Develop narratives

Write a brief, three-sentence narrative for each career accomplishment listed above. Select the best example where that accomplishment was the essential element in making the event happen. First, state what you did, second, who you did it for, and third, describe the results.

Next, write a second three-sentence narrative for each career accomplishment. Select an example from another time (a three to five year spread is best) or place.

Finish by writing a third three-sentence accomplishment narrative for each of your accomplishments. This time, you might pick a good example from a non-paying job, or perhaps a voluntary contribution.

1.a _____

_____

_____

_____

_____

1.b _____

_____

_____

_____

_____

1.c _____

_____

_____

_____

_____

2.a _____

_____

_____

_____

_____

continued next page

2.b _____

_____

_____

_____

_____

_____

2.c _____

_____

_____

_____

_____

_____

3.a _____

_____

_____

_____

_____

3.b _____

_____

_____

_____

_____

3.c

4.a

4.b

4.c

continued next page

5.a _____

_____

_____

_____

_____

5.b _____

_____

_____

_____

_____

5.c _____

_____

_____

_____

_____

As you prepare to develop your key accomplishment narratives for CASI, refer to the following list of "action words". This is by no means a definitive list, but begin by reviewing it and using the type of descriptive words you find. Don't feel limited by it—use whatever language best describes your achievements.

Management Skills: administered, analyzed, assigned, attained, chaired, consolidated, contracted, coordinated, delegated, developed, directed, eliminated, evaluated, executed, headed, improved, increased, innovated, launched, organized, oversaw, planned, prioritized, produced, recommended, reorganized, reviewed, scheduled, streamlined, strengthened, supervised, unified.

Communication Skills: addressed, arbitrated, arranged, authored, collaborated, convinced, corresponded, delivered, developed, directed, drafted, edited, enlisted, exhibited, formulated, influenced, interpreted, lectured, mediated, moderated, negotiated, persuaded, promoted, provided, publicized, reconciled, recruited, sold, spoke, translated, tripled, won, wrote.

Research Skills: clarified, collected, conducted, critiqued, diagnosed, evaluated, examined, extracted, identified, inspected, interpreted, interviewed, investigated, organized, reviewed, summarized, surveyed, systematized, uncovered.

Technical Skills: accelerated, assembled, built, calculated, computed, converted, designed, devised, engineered, fabricated, innovated, installed, maintained, operated, overhauled, programmed, remodeled, repaired, solved, upgraded.

Financial Skills: administered, allocated, analyzed, appraised, audited, balanced, budgeted, calculated, computed, converted, designed, developed, forecasted, managed, marketed, organized, planned, projected, researched.

Clerical or Detail Skills: approved, arranged, catalogued, classified, collected, compiled, delivered, dispatched, executed, generated, implemented, inspected, kept track, monitored, operated, organized, prepared, processed, provided, purchased, recorded, retrieved, screened, specified, supported, systematized, tabulated, validated, verified.

Creative Skills: acted, conceived, conceptualized, created, customized, designed, developed, directed, eliminated, established, fashioned, founded, illustrated, initiated, innovated, integrated, introduced, invented, launched, originated, performed, planned, revitalized, shaped, simplified, streamlined, wrote.

Teaching Skills: adapted, advised, clarified, coached, codified, communicated, coordinated, created, demystified, developed, enabled, encouraged, evaluated, explained, facilitated, guided, informed, innovated, instilled, instructed, persuaded, set goals, simplified, stimulated, trained, taught, wrote.

Helping Skills: assessed, assisted, clarified, coached, counseled, delivered, demonstrated, diagnosed, educated, enabled, encouraged, exhibited, expedited, facilitated, familiarized, guided, motivated, referred, rehabilitated.

Achievement Verbs: accomplished, attained, achieved, carried out, completed, consummated, expanded, finished, fulfilled, improved, obtained, pioneered, realized, reached, reduced (losses), resolved, restored, spearheaded, succeeded.

Assessment: assignment four

Analyze the data

What knowledge, skills and abilities
do you want to use in the next phase of your career?

_____

_____

_____

_____

_____

_____

What successes have you had in using
this set of knowledge, skills and abilities?

_____

_____

_____

_____

_____

_____

In the job market, where might this set of
knowledge, skills and abilities be valued?

_____

_____

_____

_____

02 Research

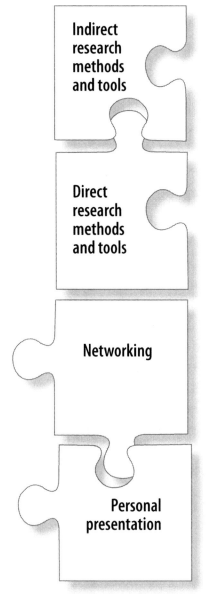

Indirect research methods and tools

Direct research methods and tools

Networking

Personal presentation

"Research is creating new knowledge."
Neil Armstrong

I Want You to Want Me

Now that you have a better understanding of who you are and what you want, it's time to find out who wants you. You are ready to take step two of the ARMS process: Research.

A thorough examination of any career position will include direct and indirect research. In relation to your career search, direct research involves gathering information through informational interviews and networking events, learning directly from people who are currently doing the type of work you're interested in. Indirect research consists of using research tools available both online and in print. This is the kind of research you did in school to prepare a report or research paper.

In this chapter, we will take an in-depth look at some of the more common tools and methods utilized in each. The most effective research utilizes a combination of both. Written job descriptions gathered doing indirect research provide a guideline from which to begin deeper exploration. Information gathered through direct research will give the job seeker insights into the actual day-to-day activities involved in a particular position, and will also reveal how the details of a position may vary among different industries. These direct and indirect methods of research can be applied to your search for company information, to further develop contacts for interviews and any other aspect of your career search. Focus your research on the particular needs you have and use these tools to gather information.

Don't think that it is always necessary to do direct research before indirect research. In fact, for our purposes, it will be more beneficial to do some time at the library and online before speaking with professionals in the field, so that you will be better prepared to make the most of their time and yours. Therefore, let's begin with a look at indirect research tools.

INDIRECT RESEARCH METHODS AND TOOLS

Researching occupational titles

Today there are two basic resources for exploring occupational titles and descriptions for job families. These are the Occupational Outlook Handbook and the O*NET Dictionary of Occupational Titles. Both of these resources are provided by the U. S. Department of Labor and are available online.

The Occupational Outlook Handbook (OOH)

This resource is available in book form through your local library and is also available online at www.bls.gov/oco/home.htm. The OOH provides detailed descriptions of roughly 88 percent of the jobs found in the U.S. today. It is updated every two years, and includes a description of the nature of the work, working conditions, training and education needed, job outlook, earnings, related jobs, and sources of additional information. Jobs in the OOH are grouped in clusters of related jobs, which will allow you to explore jobs in general groups that might be of interest.

The O*NET Dictionary of Occupational Titles (O*NET)

There is a second career database provided by the U.S. Department of Labor, known as the Occupational Information Network (O*NET), available online at www.online.onetcenter.org. This database is continuously updated and includes information on nearly 95 percent of the occupations held in the U.S. today. It can be searched by occupation, including job families and high growth industries. The O*Net can also be searched by matching skills to the positions that most often utilize them. This is a helpful tool for job seekers who have already identified which past career accomplishments they want to use in their next career position.

In addition, the O*NET has information based on personality type. The O*NET uses the Six Personality Type classifications system developed by Dr. John Holland and available in a career inventory known as the Self-Directed Search (SDS)and is available online at www.self-directed-search.com. These Six Personality Types are portrayed in the "World of Work" chart, and include: Artistic, Conventional, Enterprising, Investigative, Realistic, and Social. These can also be cross-referenced to the Strong-Campbell Interest Inventory, the Armed Services Vocational Battery, and match up nicely with the Myers-Briggs Type Indicator.

FOUR IDEAS FOR GETTING THE MOST OUT OF INDIRECT RESEARCH:

Indirect research is useful for researching classifications, jobs titles, and field-of-work opportunities. The databases provided online all have searchable functions, which can be cross-referenced by personality inventory, to former job functions and your career accomplishments.

To determine salary range. Talking about salary requirements can be a hard part of any interview. You should try to avoid answering this question directly, as it could lead to a low salary. However, if you place your requirements too high, you may disqualify yourself from the job. With proper research, you can say that you are aware that this type of job usually has a salary range from X to Y, and you can then ask if that is within the range they have in mind.

To prepare for interviews. You can let your potential employer know that you have a broad understanding of the complete scope of the job by noting the skills and other attributes listed in the research resources. From there you can provide specific examples that support your ability to handle the job, which will give you an edge in the interviewing process.

To prepare resumes and other marketing materials. The descriptions provided in these resources include skills and aptitudes used for a specific job. You can use the language provided in these resources in order to substantiate your transferable skills, experiences, and successes.

DIRECT RESEARCH METHODS AND TOOLS

Going to the source

The research tools listed above provide a general background for most occupational functions in the U.S. today. They are, however, a limited representation of the actual job. Each job will have varying responsibilities and will provide different opportunities based upon several additional factors such as industry, size of the company, and the state of the local and national economy. A more revealing method for determining job fit is to meet directly with people who are currently employed in the fields of your interest. Only by talking with current job holders will the job seeker find out the truth about the day-to-day realities of a particular occupation.

Two methods are recommended for gathering information directly from persons performing a job. These are the informational interview and participation in networking groups.

Informational Interviews

Informational Interviews are used to gather information about a position, company, or industry. Even busy professionals are often willing to give time to people who show an interest in what they are doing, provided that the person requesting the interview conducts it appropriately.

Your goals for informational interviews may change as your marketing campaign unfolds. Early in the process, you will be seeking general information relating to the positions and industries in which you have an interest. Later you will use the information you gathered to take your questions to a deeper level. This allows you to show your knowledge of the position, while gathering more information pertinent to a specific job or company.

Good question!

Here are some examples of specific questions you might ask in an informational interview. Don't feel that you are limited to these, or feel obligated to ask each and every one of them. Your goal is to uncover needs and opportunities for which you can produce solutions, so whatever inquiries you can come up with that address those issues will be appropriate.

- What is your role in this company?

- How long have you been here?

- What is your background? Training? Education?

- How does this company maintain the workforce during an economic downturn?

- What can you tell me about the way "Position X" has historically been performed?

- What improvements would you like to see happen?

- How would you describe the culture of this company?

- What are the challenges a person would face in "Position X" during the first 90 days on the job?

- Could you tell me about the stress level in this company/position? What do people do to relieve that stress?

- How would you describe your management style?

- What qualities does it take to get this job done?

- What are the most difficult issues facing your industry in the next five years?

- What solutions have you tried? Results?

INFORMATIONAL INTERVIEWS: DO'S AND DON'TS

- DO get a referral from a friend or colleague whenever possible. This will help open the door to the person granting the interview.

- DO ask if you can keep notes, but stay engaged in the conversation.

- DO approach the professional as the expert in their field. Ask them questions about how they got the position and what they do. Make inquiries about the industry in general. Ask how they like their work, as well as what they dislike about the job.

- DO ask for referrals. Since they are the experts in their field, they will know other people who may be willing to grant you an informational interview in order for you to learn more. At the end of the interview ask if they know of anyone else you should get in touch with. Often they will offer to introduce you as well.

- DO remember to be gracious. After the interview always follow up with a thank you note. This must not include your resume. Graciousness on your part shows that you really do appreciate the time they shared with you. Remember, you may want to get a referral from them or meet with them again, later in your job search.

- DON'T bring your resume. Remember, you are not asking for a job. If they ask you for a copy of your resume, tell them you will send it to them, and do so via email or "snail mail" the same day as the interview.

- DON'T ask for a job. That is not the purpose of the informational interview. If you do ask for a job, be prepared to have the door shut on you, never to be opened again.

- DON'T forget that people you interview are busy people. Ask for an interview of fifteen to twenty minutes, and stick to it! At the end of the twenty minutes, excuse yourself and thank them for taking time out of their schedule to meet with you. If they have the time, many people will extend your meeting, but this is only to be done at their discretion, not yours.

NETWORKING

For some people, attending a networking event can be intimidating. There are so many people, it can be difficult to know where to begin. If you have an introverted personality you may feel uncomfortable at the expectation of having to talk to everyone. Some people think the goal is to "collect as many business cards as possible." But what good is that, really? The good news is that you don't have to talk to everyone at a networking event. Developing a strategy for how you will work the room, including who you will talk to and how you will follow up with them will help you be more successful and have more fun at these events.

Here are 5 easy steps you can follow:

Plan ahead

Ask the facilitator ahead of time for a list of attendees & plan out who you want to make sure you meet. You may have a list of specific names, or a more generic list of people who work at a specific company, or in a particular position. If you can't get a list ahead of time, at least be sure to get to the event early and scan the name badges.

Set Goals

Make your goals specific and measurable. Determine who you need to meet and have a goal for what you are going to ask for and offer. Remember, a networking event is not the place to sell yourself. You want a referral or the opportunity to set a meeting at a later date. The most important thing to do at a networking meeting is to determine what you can do for the other person. If you think first about helping meet the other person's needs, it will help take the pressure off of you having to talk about yourself.

Document

Write the referral information on the business card (as well as the date you met the referrer, etc). Be sure to use the name of the person who referred you when contacting the referral. Be sure to offer them access to your own network. One way to do this is to ask, "Who would you like to meet that I can introduce you to at this meeting?"

Disengage

Acknowledge that this is a strange way to meet people, but that you are confined by the process. Disengaging professionally will make a big impression on the people you meet at the event. You can say something like, "If you are like me, you probably have several people you need to meet tonight. Thank you for your time. Talk to you later." Then move on to the next person!

Follow up

If you have done a good job of planning ahead, you will know the two or three people with whom you will need to follow up with the next day or the next week. Be sure to follow up promptly with the people you have identified as your target group.

You will note that only steps three and four are activities that happen at the event itself. Being strategic about your networking includes proper planning and attentive follow up.

Online Networking

The internet has fundamentally changed the ways we connect with and relate to each other. You may already be aware of, and participate in, some social networking groups such as MySpace (www.myspace.com) and Facebook (www.facebook.com). Other professional groups are using the internet to provide great social networking opportunities. Currently LinkedIn (www.linkedin.com) is one of the most popular sites for business professionals. Internet forums related to your profession, or desired profession, can also be a great resource. However, before you run out and join one of these networks, here are a few things to consider:

- Visit a site several times before you join. Make sure that the group is a good fit.

- Take the time to familiarize yourself with the FAQs , agreements, and culture of the website. You don't want to defeat the purpose of joining by doing something that irks other participants.

- Set your own standards for who you will invite to connect with. You should start by connecting with people you already know. Remember, your network becomes an extension of you.

- Don't just lurk...participate! Add value to the group. This will allow others to get to know you.

PERSONAL PRESENTATION

It may go without saying, but it is extremely important to present a professional manner during the career marketing process. Your personal appearance, how you distribute contact information, your internet presence and phone mannerisms, all communicate to others what type of an employee you might be, so make sure these things reflect your goals.

Dress

It is entirely possible that you could conduct an informational interview on Friday morning and run into the same person at the grocery store on Saturday morning. You would not dress in your most comfortable (and most ragged) sweat pants for an interview, so why would you want that person to see you dressed that way at the store? Not that you have to dress up to go grocery shopping, but while you are marketing yourself for a new career, you should always be aware of how you are presenting yourself.

Business cards

You will be asked for your contact information hundreds of times throughout the career marketing process. It is helpful to have basic business cards printed up with your name, email address and phone number. You should have an ample supply of these on your person at all times.

Online presence

More will be said about developing your online presence throughout this book. Suffice it to say that you always want to be in control of how you are perceived, even on the internet. Get a professional-sounding email address from Yahoo, Gmail, or one of the other services. "Bikerdude", "partygirl69", and "lovetosurf" should be reserved for personal use.

Phone etiquette

Does your voicemail sound like you just rolled out of bed? Do you answer the phone with a gruff or surly disposition? If so, you may want to make some changes.

To summarize, during the career marketing process, you want to present a professional appearance at all times and in all ways. Be thorough in rooting out non-professional habits that may sabotage your campaign. All it takes is one misspelled word, one shabby presentation, or one unruly phone call to make a potential employer toss your material straight into the "no" pile.

RESEARCH SUMMARY

You have now completed the Assessment and Research phases of the ARMS program. At this point you should be able to write a clear, concise career position objective for your job search, such as in the exercise that follows. Do not expect it to be perfect. This is only where you begin the marketing process. This initial description of your career position objective will give you a starting point from which to begin a more focused approach to completing applications, interviewing and networking.

In the next two chapters you will build on the foundation you have developed in the first two chapters of this book. Review the material in front of you. Refine it. Make certain that it describes you and your objectives at this time in your life.

FUTURE USES

Perhaps the most valuable future use you will get out of the work you have done in this chapter is through the contacts you make during your informational interviews. Now that you know one another, you are part of each other's network, and you are likely to cross paths again in the future. If you've made a good impression now, that can only help open doors for you in the future. As you proceed to the Marketing phase of the ARMS process, you can also use this information to help match your marketing materials to the needs of potential employers. Finally, the information you have gained can help give you a road map for your career path, well beyond the entry point you are now seeking. Keep this in mind as your career develops.

Research: assignment one

Exploring the O*net

- Log on to the O*NET website (www.online.onetcenter.org).
- Click on the "Find Occupations" tab on the left hand side.
- Enter key words from your CAREER ACCOMPLISHMENTS list.
- List below the occupations that you want to research further.

Job title _____

Median Income _____

Specific needs or training _____

Projected Growth _____

Job title _____

Median Income _____

Specific needs or training _____

Projected Growth _____

Job title _____

Median Income _____

Specific needs or training _____

Projected Growth _____

Job title _____

Median Income _____

Specific needs or training _____

Projected Growth _____

Job title _____

Median Income _____

Specific needs or training _____

Projected Growth _____

Job title _____

Median Income _____

Specific needs or training _____

Projected Growth _____

Exploring the Occupational Outlook Handbook

- Log on to the OOH website (www.bls.gov/oco).
- Search based on the data from your career accomplishments list.
- Compare with the information from the O*Net site.

Job title _____
Median Income _____
Specific needs or training _____
Projected Growth _____

Job title _____
Median Income _____
Specific needs or training _____
Projected Growth _____

Job title _____
Median Income _____
Specific needs or training _____
Projected Growth _____

Job title _____
Median Income _____
Specific needs or training _____
Projected Growth _____

Job title _____
Median Income _____
Specific needs or training _____
Projected Growth _____

Job title _____
Median Income _____
Specific needs or training _____
Projected Growth _____

Research: assignment two

Contacts list

Based on your research in assignment one, select two or three career positions you would like to research further. Then list people you know in these fields who might give you an informational interview, or who can refer you to someone in the target field. Include contact information.

target position	who I know	who they know

Keeping track

Keep a record of who you have contacted, the date you met with them, the outcome of the meeting, and any follow-up activities, including a letter of thanks for their time.

person	date	outcome	follow-up	thanks

Research: assignment three

Networking groups

Find out what sort of professional and social groups the members of your target position belong to by doing an online search. Make a note of upcoming meetings and prepare to attend them.

position	professional or social groups	meetings

Research: assignment four

Developing your image

Consider the various aspects of the impression you make on potential employers through such things as the way you dress, your online and telephone presence. Keep track of these and other areas that could use improvement and what you are doing to develop them.

aspect	status	completed
wardrobe		
professional email		
business cards		
voicemail		
ringtone		
MySpace		
LinkedIn		
personal website		
Google presence		
other		

Research: assignment five

Assembling information

Based on the information you gathered in earlier exercises, answer the following questions to help you define the career position that would be most rewarding.

What do your career accomplishments say about your next position?

_____

_____

What does feedback from others tell you to consider?

_____

_____

What does your personality inventory suggest about your next position?

_____

_____

What OOH and O*NET positions are you interested in?

_____

_____

_____

_____

Research: assignment six

Describe your career position

You will now describe your next career position, in a number of different ways, to develop your objective.

Write a ten-word description of your perfect job (this need not be a job title).

_____

_____

How would you describe this job simply, to your grandmother, for example?

_____

_____

_____

_____

How would you describe this position to a professional in that field?

_____

_____

_____

_____

Now give as inclusive a description of this position as possible. Include such things as salary, benefits, travel opportunities and obligations, insurance, and any other considerations that are important to you.

_____

_____

_____

_____

_____

_____

_____

_____

_____

_____

_____

What examples will you use to show that you can do this job?

_____

_____

_____

_____

_____

_____

03 Marketing Materials

Two sides
of the desk

The resume

Other
self-marketing
materials

Verbal profiles

"Regardless of age, regardless of position, regardless of the business we happen to be in, all of us need to understand the importance of branding. We are CEOs of our own companies: Me, Inc. To be in business today, our most important job is to be head marketer for the brand called You."

Tom Peters

Marketing and you

Though you may not realize it, you've already accomplished the first two phases of your marketing campaign: defining the product and researching who needs the product. In Assessment, you defined yourself as the product, delineated your accomplishments, quantified your past successes, described your training, and explained your professional skills. You emphasized your strengths and achievements, because they are the criteria that most employers consider to be the best predictors of your future performance. In Research, you addressed the second phase by exploring the job market, to find out where your abilities are most highly valued.

In this chapter you will develop the materials you will be using to promote yourself during your job search. They come in many shapes and sizes, some of which will be familiar to you, while others may be new. All have the same goal of advertising who you are and what you're capable of.

This message can be communicated in a variety of ways, such as conventional and electronic resumes, Curriculum Vitae, brag books, portfolios, capabilities statements, business cards and electronic networking. You also want to be prepared to promote yourself in person through what you say about yourself. All of these materials are designed to tell or show employers what you want (your career objective), that your goal is reasonable, based on your experience (your qualifications), and where you gained these capabilities (your experience and education). They also relate your strengths to the employer's needs and provide focus points in an interview.

Clearly communicating who you are and what you can contribute will set you apart from your competition. Remember, you will be interviewing with several hiring managers who may not recruit or hire people very often. If you can present yourself in a manner that meets the needs of that manager, then you will stand out among the dozens of applicants they are interviewing. As such, you will be a unique professional offering valuable solutions to the business problems faced by your potential employer. In this way, rather than being just another applicant, you become a consultant to the hiring manager. Because you offer a unique solution, your odds of getting the job increase, and so does your value to the company, which will impact your salary in all the best ways!

TWO SIDES OF THE DESK

Your self-marketing materials present you to potential employers, future colleagues, and networking groups. These documents serve a different purpose for job seekers than they do for employers. In order for you to develop these materials effectively, it is necessary to understand their purposes from both sides.

The job seeker's perspective

Many job seekers think they know how to conduct a job search. They begin with a well-written resume produced on high quality paper, send it to as many potential employers as possible and hope for the best. This is an ineffective job search method. If you have tried it, you know!

Consider this: only one interview takes place for every hundred resumes that a company receives. Furthermore, the average company conducts five to ten interviews before it makes a job offer. A quick calculation will show that there is often only one job offered for every 500 resumes received! What are your odds of being that one? If you are relying only on your resume, chances are high that you will be one of the 499 who does not get the job.

If you want to work smarter, not harder, you will conduct a marketing campaign that will make you stand out from the competition. Remember, your resume is not the product. You are the product, and the resume's job is to promote you. It does so by advertising your availability and provides proof of your qualifications to fill a given role. Like any good ad, an effective resume should provide just enough information to entice the reader to contact you for more information.

The employer's perspective

Employers receive hundreds of resumes for each advertised position, which are typically sorted into three piles: "yes", "no" and "maybe". From an employer's point of view, resumes are used as screening devices to cull unqualified applicants from the pool of candidates who will be invited for face-to-face interviews.

At this stage, employers are trying to answer the question: "Why should I hire this person?" In doing so, they also are considering a parallel question: "Are there any reasons not to?" Any red flags will result in your resume being put into the "no" pile — never again to be seen by human eyes! What will you do to make sure yours gets past that initial screening? In other words, what can you do to keep your resume from being lumped in with the "nos", bypasses the "maybes" and goes into the "yes" pile?

A better way

The job search process outlined above can be frustrating to both job-seeker and employer alike, as you must know, if you've been on either side of the applying/hiring desk. Fortunately for you and your future employer, there is a better way.

For over 60 years, professional career coaches have helped executives and managers tap the "hidden job market" by training them how to conduct a campaign to market their strengths and accomplishments to potential employers. The career marketing campaign creates a win-win situation for both the job-seeker and the employer!

With this in mind, you are ready to consider how best to assemble the work you've already done into materials to get your foot in the door of the hidden job market.

One size does not fit all.
Resumes and other marketing materials are developed to highlight your abilities in order to gain an interview. It's important to target the material to meet the needs of the employer you are talking with at the time. A well-designed, highly targeted marketing campaign is more like a laser beam than a shotgun. It will be direct and specific, accurately hitting your target, rather than taking the scattered approach typical of many job seekers.

THE RESUME

Traditionally, the resume has been the lone gun in the career seeker's arsenal. Though that approach is outdated, the resume itself is still a key component of your marketing materials. The resume hasn't gone the way of the dinosaur. Rather, the way it is to be used has evolved.

Remember, your resume is a tool in your career marketing campaign. Alone, it will not get you the position. It will eliminate you more often than it will open doors on its own merit. However, once you succeed in getting the doors opened, a well-crafted resume can support you.

Conventional resume formats:

The chronological resume

The chronological resume is perhaps the most familiar format. Organized with the most recent position first, this type of resume emphasizes dates, employers, and positions.

By quickly reviewing employment dates, the employer gets an indication of your patterns of behavior. At a glance, they can see your level of experience and skills, how long you normally stay with an employer, and whether or not your career demonstrates a pattern of advancement.

If your employment history is one of stability and progress, and if you plan on staying in the same industry or job position, a resume of this type will nicely showcase your career progression. However, if you have little work experience, frequent job changes, or employment gaps, or if you wish to change professions, a chronological resume would not be the best choice for you.

Recruiters love chronological resumes! Their job is to fill position "X". If a person has been in positions "T", "U", "V", and "W", chances are "X" will be a good fit.

EDGAR MYERS

12345 NW Main St. • Anywhere, OR 97201
555.555.5555 • email@nodomain.com • www.nodomain.com

MANAGEMENT / BRAND / MARKETING:
Brand & Marketing Strategy Development, Brand & Product Management

Enthusiastic branding specialist with experience in customer research, insights application, and strategy development. Combines expert brand application abilities with a keen, strategic mind-set to orchestrate message development and deployment. Strong reputation for completing work on time and exceeding expectations. Known for high energy, a passion for performance, and an approachable management style.

Brand Equity Measurement • Brand Management • Consumer Insight Research • Product Development/Design
Brand Strength Analysis/Benchmarking • Strategic Planning • Project Management • Client Acquisition

---

PROFESSIONAL EXPERIENCE

THE BRAND SHOP • Somewhere, WA • January 2008 - April 2008
Consulting agency focused on clients in the high-tech, health care, and non-profit sectors

Intern
Maintained client and portfolio databases. Conducted research on workflow management processes and tools. Evaluated proprietary brand equity benchmarking techniques across industry standards. Consulted for naming and brand strategy projects.

Key Highlights
- Drafted estimates and proposals directly resulting in no less than $100,000 of new contracts
- Conducted phone-interview research domestically and internationally for client projects

ANYWHERE STATE UNIVERSITY • Anywhere, OR • January 2007 - August 2007
Public university serving over 24,000 undergraduate and graduate students

Research Consultant
Collected reports and documentation on over 150 multinational companies for ongoing research project on corporate responsibility. Read and analyzed related reporting practices and reported trends and report qualities to principal researchers.

ACTION SPORTS • Anywhere, OR • February 2007 - August 2007
Subsidiary of Wilson Sporting Goods - manufacturer of high-end softball and baseball equipment

External Consultant
Conducted market research on consumer trends in Japanese baseball. Tested products multiple individuals-focusing on product performance, quality, and product management efforts. Developed strategies for marketing to players of rubber baseball in Japan.

EDUCATION

MASTER OF INTERNATIONAL MANAGEMENT • Global Marketing
Anywhere State University • Anywhere, OR

BACHELOR OF SCIENCE • Political Science
University of Nowhere • Nowhere, OR

BACHELOR OF SCIENCE • Physics / Mathematics
University of Nowhere • Nowhere, OR

The functional resume

Functional resumes de-emphasize employment dates, employers, and responsibilities. Organized primarily to communicate qualifications, skills, and accomplishments, this format may or may not reference particular jobs or employers. With its focus on abilities and transferable skills, individuals with little direct work experience, or those seeking to make a major career change, often use this type of resume.

Functional resumes tend to raise red flags for recruiters who have learned to read between the lines. While the functional resume's major strength is its focus on skills and accomplishments, this strength also becomes a weakness when it is not accompanied by references to specific employers, job titles, and inclusive employment dates.

Employers may be suspicious of candidates presenting functional resumes, assuming that they may be concealing their lack of direct work experience, an unstable work history, or a less-than-stellar pattern of career advancement.

The five second rule
A resume may be viewed by a hiring manager, recruiter, or HR staff member for as little as five seconds before it is put in the "no" pile. Therefore, it is critical that your key accomplishment narratives stand out.

John R. Patrick

Home (903) 641-2212   Cell (903) 247-5555   Email: JRPEmail@googlemail.com

OBJECTIVE

To obtain a Human Resource management position in a growing organization that utilizes my proven skills of recruiting, training, motivating and deploying people to:

- Increase organizational performance through recruitment and retention of personnel.
- Develop and maintain HR functions.
- Train and develop employees to maximize the strategic use of human resources.

QUALIFICATIONS

Over 5 years of successful experience and expertise in:

- **Recruiting and Hiring**
- **Organizing People and Processes**
- **Training and Developing**

ACHIEVEMENTS

RECRUITED, TRAINED and MANAGED team of multi-national personnel in developing a marketing strategy to extend US software company into international markets.
Results: Small US software company was able to expand operations into international arena, increasing international sales from $0 to $150,000 in six months.

TRAINED and MOTIVATED co-worker to achieve a high level of success.
Results: Trainee improved her production by 20%, which allowed her to be promoted to a management position where she subsequently was responsible for training and motivating her team to start 468 students ($11.7 million booked revenue).

PLANNED and IMPLEMENTED monthly training program for startup organization.
Results: Grew leadership team for nonprofit organization from 0 to 25 strong leaders, which led to the growth of the organization from 2 to 85 active participants within 2 years.

ORGANIZED purchase and administration of new database system for ABCDO.
Results: More than 40% reduction in production costs.

LED PEOPLE to increase nonprofit organization's membership by conducting SWOT analysis and focusing on strategic goals through involvement and retention of young families with children.
Results: 50% increase in participation of young families with children resulting in increased weekly attendance.

EDUCATION, PROFESSIONAL CERTIFICATIONS AND MEMBERSHIP

Master of Business Administration	Cleveland State University
Bachelor of Arts in Social Work	West Liberty State College, West Liberty, WVA
Certificate of Human Resource Management	Cleveland State University
American Society for Training and Development (ASTD)	Ohio Chapter, Cleveland, OH
Toastmasters International	Club 42669, Cleveland OH

The hybrid resume

The hybrid resume combines the best elements of the chronological and functional resume formats. This type of resume primarily emphasizes your objectives, skills, and accomplishments, but also includes a chronological employment history.

YOUR RESUME: A $350,000 INVESTMENT

How much do you expect to make in your next job? Fifty thousand a year? Seventy? A hundred thousand or more? Multiply that by the number of years you plan to spend on the job, and that's how much your resume is worth! If you were going to buy space in the New York Times or Wall Street Journal for an ad campaign that would yield you this much revenue, wouldn't you want to make sure you got it right? Here are four tips to make sure your resume does its job so you can do yours.

Quantify results.
The "native language" of the people who have the authority to hire you is numbers. In order to best speak their language and gain their attention you need to quantify your results from past activities. How much? How Many? When? Where? How often? How much of an increase was that? These numbers will show your potential employer that you have done it before and can do it again for them.

Don't waste space!
Would you put a picture of your dog in a full page ad in the New York Times? Not unless you are selling puppies! Then why list your hobbies and accomplishments unless they are directly related to your career objective?

Be clear about what you have to offer.
Don't make the reader guess. Don't force them to read between the lines. If you can do something for them, state it up front.

Focus your product offering.
Know what you have to offer and who needs it. DON'T try to be all things to all people. Focus your USP (Unique Selling Proposition) to present yourself in the best way to your key target audience.

Alex B. Brendland

Tel: 360-555-2212
e-mail: Alex_Brendland@coolmail.com

Skills Summary

Branded product marketer with extensive experience in regional, national and international markets. Strategic and tactical marketing planner, successful in implementing results-oriented management principles. Managed and coordinated marketing promotions in 17 different countries. Seasoned writer and editor.

Qualifications

Program Management	**Advertising**	**Editing**
Strategic Planning	**Public Relations**	**Project Planning**

Achievements

- Managed USGA export program that provided marketing assistance to hundreds of industry firms. **Result:** Doubled program budget from $4.8 million to $10 million in four years.
- Created new design for exhibition stand for use at the world's largest food show held in Europe. Developed theme and recruited companies to participate in the event. Developed an advertising strategy that generated publicity for the industry in conjunction with show. **Results:** Achieved 100% satisfaction rate from participating exhibitors. American Ambassador to Switzerland used our pavilion for his press opportunity – twice.
- Developed promotional materials, featuring logos from various promotional partners, for electronic distribution and for use at major trade shows. Designed advertisements, timed to coincide with the same trade shows, for publication in trade magazines. **Result:** Heightened trade awareness led to $1 million increase in sales for industry participants.
- Briefed press on trade association, its activities, and success stories. **Result:** Generated free publicity for organization in trade magazines and newspapers including *The Capitol Press, American Taste Magazine,* and *Exporter Journal.*

Work Experience

Marketing Manager Ready-Set-Go Fine Foods 2007 – current
- Manage export sales for trading company. Respond to trade leads. Buy products; quote pricing to buyers. Oversee invoicing and transportation logistics. **Result:** Secured new importer/distributor in Beijing, China.

Writer/Editor American Food Magazine 2007 – current
- Write articles promoting brands and companies across the US in European markets. **Results:** Since joining the magazine it has become the industry leader.

Brand Manager Western Farmer's Trade Association 2002 – 2007
- Managed Federal marketing program on behalf of 8-state region. **Result:** Increased program participation from 160 companies to 230 companies within 5 years (44%).
- Consulted with companies on how to leverage marketing resources. **Result:** Helped small-sized bagel producer in Idaho save $30,000 with a one-hour phone conversation.
- Supervised staff of three full-time employees.

Generic Brand Manager Western U.S. Agricultural Trade Association 1987 – 2001
- Administered 50 promotional projects per year, communicating and coordinating with project managers in 13 states and contractors in13 countries. **Result:** Increased program budget from $1.2 million to $2.8 million.

Education

- B.A. Business Studies Purdue University
- Completed overseas study at Instituto de Lenguas Classicas Barcellona, Spain

References Provided Upon Request

The E-Resume

Resumes are now commonly shared via email, as an attachment, or within the body of your text. Any resume can be converted to an electronic resume simply by saving the document in plain text and making minor formatting changes. If you are attaching your resume to an email it is best to save it as a pdf file. This way the receiver will see your resume as you sent it, no matter what computer operating system format they are using.

Effective electronic resumes should always include keywords and short phrases as they are listed in the specific job posting for which you are applying.

Monster/Jobdango Website Profile

It is important to remember that only about two percent of jobs are found on these boards. If your chances are only two out of a hundred that you will get a job this way, make sure that you spend no more than two percent of your time on them! That being said, people do find a job this way, and you may be one of them. The secret to getting seen on boards such as these is consistent updating of your materials. Go in every other day or so and make a change, even if it's only a small one, to your posting. That way it will show up as having been recently updated.

Google me, baby

Also remember, your resume is not the only representation of you that a potential employer sees. Have you "googled" yourself lately? You can be assured that a potential employer will google your name prior to offering you an interview. What does your web profile say about you as a potential employee?

OTHER SELF-MARKETING MATERIALS

Curriculum Vitae (CV)

Curriculum Vitae is Latin for "course of life". Also commonly referred to as CVs or Vitaes, they are most often used by jobseekers pursuing positions in academic, medical, legal, scientific, or religious fields. More formal than a chronological, functional, or hybrid resume, a CV is at least two pages but it could very easily become longer if the candidate is highly experienced and has a substantial record of professional publication.

This detailed document usually includes publications, presentations, professional activities, patent and copyright history, grants, projects, honors, awards, and additional professional achievement information.

Portfolio

Portfolios are generally used as a means to present samples of creative production. Public relations and marketing professionals, writers, corporate trainers, educators, consultants, graphic designers, artists, models, and actors use portfolios to showcase their work. The portfolio should represent a collection of the client's best work, as it relates to the desired position. In addition to showcasing samples of work, it should also include a one or two-page chronological or hybrid resume, as well as any available press materials that highlight career accomplishments.

Since a portfolio could consist of many pages, a sample is not included here. Numerous examples are available online, so if you feel this format is for you, do a search for "example portfolios" to see what others in your intended field have produced.

Brag Book

A brag book is similar to a portfolio in that it may contain samples of your work, photos, recommendation letters, or anything else that will showcase your talents and help a potential employer see that you are capable of doing the job for them.

Some have been created in the form of a brochure that can be left with the interviewer following the meeting. Others are presented in a three-ring binder and are intended to remain with the job seeker.

Capabilities statement

The capabilities statement is much shorter and less detailed than a resume. The one-page document defines your skills and what you can do for a company. It is designed to highlight your achievements and should include a brief clarifying statement indicating how those skills will be applied in the future.

This kind of documentation has been used successfully by recent college graduates with limited or no experience, persons seeking to change functions within the same industry, as well as those seeking to switch industries, but keep the same function.

For each category included in your capabilities statement, you should provide at least three examples of your abilities.

Decisions, decisions

Often, people wonder which resume format is best. For most clients, the hybrid resume is recommended as a starting point. In the end, however, the opinion that matters the most is that of the hiring manager. They are the one who has the job and who will make the offer based on their needs.

If you are working with a Crossroads Coach, they can advise you personally on which resume format is best for your particular circumstances. Your Career Coach will help you determine when a CV is appropriate and advise you if there are specific companies or organizations where this kind of presentation will be more effective than a standard resume.

To make an appointment with a CMS Career Crossroads Coach, or to see examples of CVs, portfolios, brag books and capabilities statements, please visit **cmscareerxroads.com**.

VERBAL PROFILES

Your "Elevator Pitch"

What you say about yourself is as important as your written marketing materials. Every day you have opportunities to introduce yourself to new people. Some of them are potential employers. Others will know potential employers. When asked about yourself, or what you do, you have a perfect opportunity to give a response that describes where you want to be in your next career position. Because circumstances will vary, you want to have a series of clear, concise statements that can be used in a variety of settings. We call these statements your "elevator pitch", because it takes about the same amount of time to tell the person about yourself as it does to ride from one floor to the next in an elevator. In fact, an elevator is a great place to practice! Your pitch must be focused and well rehearsed. Remember, you only get one chance to make a good first impression.

Your elevator pitch should answer three questions:

- What is your career objective?
- What qualifications do you have to support your career objective?
- How can this person help you achieve your objective? *(use only if appropriate).*

You'll want to have a variety of examples in your elevator pitch arsenal. These examples should include:

- A ten-word statement of your Unique Selling Proposition, or USP

- General elevator pitches of thirty and sixty seconds for initial introductions at informational interviews and networking events

- A sixty second elevator pitched customized for job interviews

- A somewhat longer version of one to three minutes to pitch at networking events

- A ten to thirty- second version for casual social encounters or when meeting someone new

- A thirty to sixty-second version for telephone conversation introductions

The good news is that most of the heavy lifting has already been done! Your presentation information is already available in the brief narratives of your CASI statements. You will begin with your ten word USP as the target, and include brief statements to support your claim. Be sure to keep your statements brief. The elevator pitch is NOT the place to go into detail. The purpose of these statements is to introduce yourself to potential employers and people who know them. We recommend you give your shortest pitch, and watch the person to whom you are talking. If their eyes light up, give them another little snippet or example. If they say something like, "That's nice. Please pass the butter," don't waste your time. Pass the butter and move on to the next person.

Always try to focus your statement on where you are going, even if you aren't quite there yet. Our brains listen to what we tell them about ourselves and pull us to become that reality. If you say you are a "marketing professional" long enough, you will find a way to become a marketing professional!

The Noodle's Four-Step Process for Writing an Elevator Pitch

Toastmaster Jim Nudelman has a simple four-step process for writing an elevator pitch. Jim ("the Noodle", as he is known to friends and family) is an experienced National Sales Trainer, so he should know something about putting your best foot forward to capitalize on a brief window of opportunity. Here's his process and finished product:

Step 1   Begin with an action phrase. Do not use a job title, but describe what you do.

For example: *I am a master of...*

Step 2   Add a one-sentence statement about what you do.

For example: *I teach sales professionals...*

Step 3   Give a statement of the specific impact of your service.

For example: *People who utilize my process have increased...*

Step 4   End with a call to action:

For example: *Please introduce me to...*

Here's Jim's elevator pitch:

"My name is Jim Nudelman. I am a master of building relationships. I teach sales professionals how to build and grow their business. Sales professionals who have attended my workshops have increased their business by as much as fifty percent. Please introduce me to people looking to build and grow their business."

To listen to examples of USPs, general elevator pitches, longer pitches for networking purposes, and telephone introductions, visit cmscareerxroads.com.

MARKETING MATERIALS SUMMARY

Your self-marketing materials are a collection of documents and verbal presentations that may include resumes, CVs, an online presence, capabilities statements, brag books, brief narratives and elevator pitches.

Each item is used as an advertisement or a calling card to entice potential employers to arrange an interview with you.

FUTURE USES

Clients have successfully used their Marketing Materials in many ways to enhance their careers. They can be used to create tracking systems for achievements, to justify a raise, promotion, or the creation of a new position. Refer to them to enhance applications for professional membership groups, business organizations or further education. Use them when preparing professional biographies for public speaking, web sites, political campaigns or book covers. When writing presentations, look to your marketing materials for stories and examples.

Marketing materials: assignment one

Develop a clear objective statement for your resume

A good objective statement should be written to encourage the reader to read the rest of your resume. Use the following formula to help you write your own.

Step one: Start with the level of responsibility you want.
"A management position…"
"An entry level position…"
"An executive position…"

Alternate step one: You may want to begin with the position title you want.
"A division director..."
"A financial consultant position…"
"Lab technician…"

Step two: Follow with the industry that suits you most .
"…in a design firm…"
"…for a language school…"
"…in the medical field…"

Step three: Insert a connecting word or phrase.
"overseeing" (for an executive position)
"utilizing" (for a "hands-on" position)
 "related to" (for a mid-level position)

Step four: Put in two or three key skills (as defined in CASI).
"designing software"
 "developing curriculum"
"photographing children"

Step five: You may want to add a geographic preference.
"…in an international firm…"
"…in Portland, Oregon…"

Step six: You may want to add something about the company.
"…a mid-sized firm…"
"…a Fortune 500 company…"

Step seven: Finish with something you can do for the company
"…to increase sales."
"…to maximize efficiency, thereby increasing profitability."

Examples

"A management position within a small, family manufacturing business that will utilize my proven ability to reduce waste and increase corporate profitability."

"Sales management position in a major international firm that involves my abilities to develop, motivate and lead teams to successfully accomplish difficult goals and objectives."

"A senior level finance manager position in a Oregon-based company requiring flexible management skills, creative problem solving and effective communication, oriented towards deadlines while maximizing the corporate bottom line."

Write your own objective statement.

_____

_____

_____

_____

_____

Marketing materials: assignment two

Keeping track of marketing materials

type	draft	completed	updated
chronological resume			
functional resume			
hybrid resume			
e-resume			
email resume (pdf)			
Monster profile			
Jobdango profile			
MySpace profile			
LinkedIn profile			
website			
CV			
portfolio			
brag book			
capabilities statement			
10-word overview			
elevator pitch			
60 second pitch			
90 second pitch			
networking pitch			
social pitch			

Marketing materials: assignment three

Define your Unique Selling Proposition

A USP is a concise statement of what sets you apart from everyone else who does the job you do.

To begin, review your key accomplishment narratives from the CASI exercises. Also, think about the people you have met in informal interviews and the language they use to describe their needs. Consider the examples given here, and see how they not only say what the person does, but what's special about the way they do it. There are more tips on refining your USP in chapter 4, Strategy, on page 75.

*"I specialize in working with thirty-nine year old women who want to
 run a marathon on their fortieth birthday."*
Chiropractor

"I recruit, train and motivate people to reach their highest potential."
Found work as a Corporate Trainer.

"My expertise is the intersection of science, business and regulatory issues."
Found work doing business development for an environmental science company.

"I love to work with difficult people."
Project Manager

Write your Unique Selling Proposition.

_____

_____

_____

_____

_____

04Strategy

It's not about you

Branded!

Project Management 101

Keeping Track

"Strategy is at once the course we chart, the journey we imagine and, at the same time, it is the course we steer, the trip we actually make. Even when we are embarking on a voyage of discovery, with no particular destination in mind, the voyage has a purpose, an outcome, an end to be kept in view."
Fred Nickols

Having evaluated yourself and the job market in steps one and two, Assessment and Research, and having prepared various materials in step three, Marketing Materials, you are now ready to take it to the streets with a Strategy!

As discussed throughout this book, networking will be one of the most important means by which you translate all of your preparations into an occupation. What is networking, and how does it help people find their perfect career? Networking is word-of-mouth marketing for job seekers, and word-of-mouth marketing is the best there is.

Buyers today are savvy to the tricks of the advertising industry. When we see a big-budget ad for a blockbuster movie, it may attract our interest. It may even make us want to see the movie. By contrast, if a friend or trusted colleague tells us how much they loved the movie, the decision is not whether to go, but when. The opposite is also true. No matter how good an advertising campaign, if our friends tell us the movie is a "dog", we are unlikely to spend the time and money to venture into the theater. This is the case with all sorts of businesses. Would you eat at a restaurant where your friends told you the food was bad, or the service poor? Word-of-mouth can effectively make or break any product, and that includes you and your career marketing campaign!

IT'S NOT ABOUT YOU

Yes, you read that correctly. Effective networking is not about you. Rather, it is about finding opportunity for the mutual benefit of two people and their extended networks. In order to be an effective networker, you must do three things:

- Listen to the needs of the person or company with whom you are speaking

- Know your networking partners and what they can offer

- Be clear about your own Unique Selling Proposition

When you meet someone for a networking meeting, you want to spend more time listening than talking. You want to get a clear picture of their needs, and how you and your network can help them meet their goals. Networking is not about you! It's about helping other people get what they need. By doing so you will activate what Brian Tracey calls ,"The Law of Reciprocity." Other people will help you get what you need, if you help them get what they want.

Having said this, to effectively offer your services, as well as draw interest to yourself, you must be able to concisely state your Unique Selling Proposition, that which sets you apart from everyone else who does your job. You have already defined your USP in the assignments in chapter three, Marketing Materials. Remember, it should be brief and targeted, and at the same time intriguing enough to entice the listener to want to know more about you.

BRANDED!

Recall that the goal of marketing is to rent out space in the mind of the consumer. Now let's consider where branding fits in. Essentially, a brand is a promise of what a product or service will deliver every time. Regarding your career goals, your brand should relate to the two things employers are most concerned about: saving money and making money

As you begin your strategic plan, you will want to keep these ideas in mind. Your strategic plan is a means of presenting your brand ("Brand You"), so that you will be able to "rent out space in the mind" of potential employers. Everything in your strategic plan should point to your USP – your brand. You do not want to put out any material that might confuse potential employers about you.

A strategic plan for promoting your brand will save you time and effort in the job search, as well as making it possible for you to obtain a higher salary. The reason for this has to do with basic economic principles. When a product is in high demand, and the supply is limited, it can fetch a higher price. Your objective is to show that you have a unique combination of skills, training, and experience, which make you, alone, capable of performing the job to the highest degree of satisfaction. If, on the other hand, your marketing materials make you look like everyone else, you would be presenting yourself as a common commodity. A commodity is something which is supplied without distinction in quality throughout the market. In other words, cotton is cotton. Wheat is wheat. On the other hand, cars come in various models from many manufacturers, and offer varying degrees of quality and performance. You don't want to be a commodity. The economic law of demand will work in your favor if you can display your uniqueness. In an era when hiring managers are barraged by three to four hundred resumes for each position, standing out is a good thing!

Here are some tips for refining your USP, the key to making you stand out in the crowd.

- As you conduct informational interviews, pay careful attention to the words that potential employers are using to describe their issues and their best workers. Use their words to describe yourself whenever possible. Your words should reflect the way your potential employers think about the best people who work for them.

- Try out different wording on different people. Pay attention to what makes their eyes light up.

- Don't be vague! We cannot say enough about the importance of being clear and concise in promoting your brand.

- Avoid clichés. Be original in stating what makes you unique.

- Focus on what you are capable of and willing to do in your next career position. Remember, you don't have to take a job you don't want, no matter how good you may be at it.

- Emphasize the future. Use examples from your past to show potential employers how you could help them solve their current and future business problems.

- Business owners and managers are concerned about two things: how you can help them make or save money. Show them you have the capability to do this for them, and they will be more likely to want to talk with you.

- Emphasize the key words and accomplishments from your CASI in chapter one.

- Trim the fat. Don't include awards and activities that do not expressly relate to your future career position.

PROJECT MANAGEMENT 101

Think of project management as organizing and following through on steps that must be completed in order to successfully complete a large project. An example could be a wedding to be held in the backyard of your house in three months time. This would be your target. There are several smaller projects (your goals) that will need to be completed, in order to have a wedding you can be proud of hosting. One aspect would be yard work. You will need to haul off a load of yard debris and collected junk. But before you can take the load to the dump, you must mow the lawn, clean out the garage, weed the flower bed, trim the hedge, and so on. Each of these smaller tasks (your objectives) can be worked on simultaneously, especially if you have teenage children to help you. Nevertheless, the smaller objectives need to be completed prior to your trip to the dump. You would do well to set benchmarks and time deadlines for each to be completed, so you can stay on track with your target of holding a wedding. In addition to the yard work that needs to be done, you will have other goals, such as planning the ceremony and reception. Clearly, a big project like this would benefit from thorough planning in the beginning, and careful monitoring throughout, to make sure all of the important aspects of the wedding come together smoothly.

PROJECT MANAGEMENT NOTE
The language of goal setting can change from place to place and industry to industry. For some industries the words "goal" and "objective" are interchangeable. For the purpose of consistency, here we will use the above. Once you understand how we are using these words, you can feel free to change the language to fit your own needs.

A simple project management framework for successfully completing a project is given below. The worksheets at the end of this chapter will help you organize and prioritize the goals and objectives that will propel you along the path from where you are towards your target of finding the perfect career position.

There are three key components to effective Project Management:

Set goals and objectives.

Goals are the big picture things you must achieve in order to reach your target. In the example above, your target is to host a wedding. Goals are the things that must be done to help you reach your target. In this case, the broad categories include: cleaning up the yard, planning the wedding ceremony, and preparing for the reception. Objectives are the tasks you will complete in order to implement your goals. Your objectives for achieving your first goal include mowing the lawn, weeding the flower bed, trimming the hedges, and so on. Another way to think about it is to see your objectives as the activities you undertake, while goals are the broad groups of activities

Establish benchmarks.

Benchmarks will help to determine if your efforts are bringing you closer to your goal in a timely fashion. Benchmarks allow you to measure your progress, so they will need to include numbers and due dates. As you prioritize the things that need to be done first, you can set specific, measurable benchmarks to help keep track of how you are doing. Let's look at our wedding for another example. If you set a benchmark of "three weeks from today" for completing the goal of planning the ceremony, you will also want to determine how many guests will attend, who is in the wedding party, how many chairs to rent, and so on. Setting benchmarks will make it possible for you to keep track of your progression, so you know where you are in your project.

Measure and manage results.

A clear plan with a means of recording progress is essential. It could be a checklist, or a spreadsheet, depending on the complexity of the project. Nevertheless, without it, essential details can easily be forgotten. Once you have set goals and objectives, and established benchmarks, it will be easy to set up a system to help you manage your project. Such a system will allow you to work on a specific area of your project without fear of missing an important detail in another area. It also gives you a sense of accomplishment and satisfaction with your progression.

KEEPING TRACK

In your career marketing campaign you will conduct a variety of interviews and attend many networking events. At each of these you will ask for, and receive, additional referrals to follow up with. You will soon find out that you have more opportunities than you can realistically handle. This is a good problem to have! It means you are on the right track. However, in order to be effective during this process, it is important to have some guidelines set up regarding where to spend your time and energy, so you can get the most return on your investment. Some of your activities will be more important than others. Some will meet your desired objectives, and some won't. Having a system to track and prioritize your activities will help you focus your efforts on the ones that are most promising for your ultimate goal of finding the perfect career.

There are three things you will want to do after each informative interview or networking event that you attend:

- Evaluate and prioritize the activity and the additional opportunities or introductions according to your objectives. Each activity, opportunity, or introduction will be sorted into one of three "buckets", labeled as high priority, medium priority, or low priority. In this way, you can focus on activities and opportunities that will be most likely to move you towards your goal, rather than going round in circles doing things that aren't getting you anywhere.

- Set follow-up activities with specific and measurable goals. You will determine the criteria, action, and frequency for following up on each item within these categories. This will keep you thinking forward about the next step, so that your progress won't stall.

- Track your results. This will keep you from covering the same ground twice, as well as ensure that you don't miss out on important details, like thanking people for their time. It also provides you with a sense of continuing progress, to keep you motivated as you come closer and closer to achieving your goals.

STRATEGY SUMMARY

In the first three steps of the ARMS process you worked towards developing the target of your career search. You learned how essential it is to develop a career marketing campaign in order to find your perfect position. That campaign is based upon your transferable knowledge, skills and abilities, in consideration of what you are capable of and willing to do in your next career position, regardless of the specific title of your prior career choices. Your career marketing campaign consists of a variety of things, including: resumes, your Internet and verbal profiles based on your Unique Selling Proposition, and other marketing materials.

In this chapter you were given a framework for putting your career marketing campaign into action based on your Unique Selling Proposition (your USP). Setting goals and objectives, establishing benchmarks, and measuring and managing results is a simple, proven project management framework that can be used throughout your career in many ways. Take the time to learn these steps now, and they will serve you well in the years to come!

FUTURE USES

These strategic planning methods can be applied to any aspect of your career, or anything else you want to accomplish. They can help you produce consistent results in order to earn a promotion at your current company. You could apply them to help your company expand into new markets, or to start your own company. Especially keep them in mind for the next time you're planning a backyard wedding!

Strategy: assignment one

Setting targets, goals and objectives

To do this assignment, you'll need some Post-it notes and a wall.

On one of the Post-it notes , write down your target, for example, a career position you want to attain.

Post it in the center of the wall.

Now, brainstorm to come up with all of the things you will need to do in order to achieve your target. Include people you will have to meet, posting your resume online, getting some dress socks. Include any aspect of the ARMS process you've learned throughout this book, as well as anything else that comes to mind that is related to achieving your target. Don't "self-edit" at this point. Just make notes of things to do.

You now have a Post-it note with a target on a wall, and a bunch of activities related to that target.

Now, around that target, put the notes that you've come up with into related groups. For example, "update resume" and "post resume online" would be posted close to one another. "Buy dress socks" and "make a trip to the dry cleaners" would go together. Each group is a goal, such as "resume" or "personal presentation".

Finally, re-order the notes according to priority. What is most important? What has to happen first? Clearly, you will want to update your resume before posting it on the internet, so it should be on top of that group. Each of the things you must do are objectives to achieving your goals.

Once you've done this with all of your notes, transfer the information to a piece of paper. At the top write down your target, and below that record all the goals and objectives in the order you must follow to achieve them. Take these objectives and use the following exercise to monitor your progress in achieving them.

Name your target

What is your target?

_____

List your goals for achieving that target.

Goal number one:

_____

_____

Goal number two:

_____

_____

Goal number three:

_____

_____

Goal number four:

_____

_____

Goal number five:

_____

_____

Goal number one: _____

To be completed by (date): _____

Goal details: _____

_____

Objectives: _____

_____

_____

_____

Benchmarks: _____

_____

_____

_____

Results: _____

_____

_____

_____

Follow-up activities: _____

_____

_____

_____

Goal number two: _____

To be completed by (date): _____

Goal details: _____

_____

Objectives: _____

_____

_____

_____

_____

Benchmarks: _____

_____

_____

_____

_____

Results: _____

_____

_____

_____

_____

Follow-up activities: _____

_____

_____

_____

continued next page

Goal number three: _____

To be completed by (date): _____

Goal details: _____

_____

Objectives: _____

_____

_____

_____

_____

Benchmarks: _____

_____

_____

_____

_____

Results: _____

_____

_____

_____

_____

Follow-up activities: _____

_____

_____

_____

Goal number four _____

To be completed by (date): _____

Goal details: _____

_____

Objectives: _____

_____

_____

_____

_____

Benchmarks: _____

_____

_____

_____

_____

Results: _____

_____

_____

_____

_____

Follow-up activities: _____

_____

_____

_____

continued next page

Goal number five _____

To be completed by (date): _____

Goal details: _____

_____

Objectives: _____

_____

_____

_____

Benchmarks: _____

_____

_____

_____

Results: _____

_____

_____

_____

Follow-up activities: _____

_____

_____

_____

Goal number (   ): _____

To be completed by (date): _____

Goal details: _____

_____

Objectives: _____

_____

_____

_____

_____

Benchmarks: _____

_____

_____

_____

_____

Results: _____

_____

_____

_____

_____

Follow-up activities: _____

_____

_____

_____

Strategy: assignment two

Prioritizing your opportunities.

Evaluate and prioritize activities and opportunities or introductions according to your objectives. Each activity, opportunity, or introduction will be sorted into one of three "buckets", labeled as high priority, medium priority, or low priority.

Into the high priority bucket, note opportunities that are directly related to your goals, and that you are prepared to follow through on. You should act on high priority bucket opportunities within the next twenty-four hours. In the medium priority bucket, put opportunities that are in some way related to your goals, and act on them sometime in the coming week. In the low priority bucket, put opportunities that seem unrelated or that you don't expect much out of. Follow up on these only once you've attended to the high and medium priority buckets. Be aware, however, that an opportunity can move from one bucket to another, based on new information, or your own personal preparedness.

Consider some examples. You want to work in the footwear industry. Someone you know has lunch on Tuesdays with the president of Nike, and has offered to introduce you. Sounds like a "high priority bucket" opportunity, doesn't it? Not if you haven't researched the company, or if you don't have a decent shirt to wear. Now your priorities become research and wardrobe, so you will be prepared to pursue this opportunity.

Or perhaps a friend of yours knows about your career goals and tells you to call his cousin, who is "really into shoes". Doesn't sound like much. But it turns out that this cousin who is "really into shoes" designs them for Gucci. What seemed a low priority item has now become high priority.

Keep track of your opportunities and the contact information for both the person who referred you and the opportunity itself. Under "plan of action", include time and date information. Be sure and thank people who open doors for you.

High priority bucket

opportunity	contact info	plan of action	thanks

Medium priority bucket

opportunity	contact info	plan of action	thanks

Low priority bucket

opportunity	contact info	plan of action	thanks

assignments example pages

Assessment: assignment one

Record personality assessment results

Which personality assessment or assessmements did you use?

I took the Keirsey
Temperament Sorter

Write a brief description of the opportunities
available to you based on what you learned from your personality profile.

It was interesting to see the
results because I didn't fit
into one profile. I was a
XSFJ which means my E and
I were equal so I show
traits from both. This test
helped me see some of my
key traits that will help
when I am trying to figure
out what kind of position
I want.

Assessment: assignment two

Send out letters of or emails of request for feedback

(see following page for example letter)

Consider the responses

According to the insights provided by friends,
relatives and co-workers, what are your major professional strengths?

Passionate, Strong listener,
confident, creative, and a
great problem solver.

Are there any weaknesses or "blind spots" that were pointed out to you?

Too quiet at times, tries to do
too many things at once

What insights have you gained from this information?

Showed me the areas I
need work in.

Timothy Bryan
2227 Townsend Way
Hollywood, FL 33020
January 19, 2008

Mr. Corbett Bise, Director
Gidgets Widgets
2625 Amistad Drive
Port St. Joe, FL 32456

Dear Mr. Bise,

I have recently engaged Career Management Solutions to assist me in my preparations for a new career. CMS uses an approach designed to focus on past achievements and successes. Part of their process is to determine the strengths, abilities and motivations of their clients. They want to see their clients as their friends see them, both the good and not so good.

Will you please write a letter in which you identify what you believe to be my strong points and my weak points, as well as what you think I need to be both successful and happy in a career. Please send your response to me at the above address at your earliest convenience.

Thank you for your
time,

Timothy Bryan

Assessment: Assignment three

Career Achievement Self Inventory (CASI)

As you prepare to develop your key accomplishment narratives for CASI, refer to the following list of "action words". This is by no means a definitive list, but begin by reviewing it and using the type of descriptive words you find. Don't feel limited by it--use whatever language best describes your achievements.

Management Skills: administered, analyzed, assigned, attained, chaired, consolidated, contracted, coordinated, delegated, developed, directed, eliminated, evaluated, executed, headed, improved, increased, innovated, launched, organized, oversaw, planned, prioritized, produced, recommended, reorganized, reviewed, scheduled, streamlined, strengthened, supervised, unified.

Communication Skills: addressed, arbitrated, arranged, authored, collaborated, convinced, corresponded, delivered, developed, directed, drafted, edited, enlisted, exhibited, formulated, influenced, interpreted, lectured, mediated, moderated, negotiated, persuaded, promoted, provided, publicized, reconciled, recruited, sold, spoke, translated, tripled, won, wrote.

Research Skills: clarified, collected, conducted, critiqued, diagnosed, evaluated, examined, extracted, identified, inspected, interpreted, interviewed, investigated, organized, reviewed, summarized, surveyed, systematized, uncovered, unraveled

Technical Skills: accelerated, assembled, built, calculated, computed, converted, designed, devised, engineered, fabricated, innovated, installed, maintained, operated, overhauled, programmed, remodeled, repaired, set up, solved, upgraded.

Financial Skills: administered, allocated, analyzed, appraised, audited, balanced, budgeted, calculated, computed, converted, cut, developed, forecasted, managed, marketed, organized, planned, projected, researched.

Clerical or Detail Skills: approved, arranged, catalogued, classified, collected, compiled, delivered, dispatched, executed, generated, implemented, inspected, kept track of, monitored, operated, organized, prepared, processed, provided, purchased, recorded, retrieved, screened, specified, supported, systematized, tabulated, validated.

Creative Skills: acted, conceived, conceptualized, created, customized, designed, developed, directed, eliminated, established, fashioned, founded, illustrated, initiated, innovated, instituted, integrated, introduced, invented, launched, originated, performed, planned, revitalized, shaped, simplified, streamlined.

Teaching Skills: adapted, advised, clarified, coached, codified, communicated, coordinated, created, demystified, developed, enabled, encouraged, evaluated, explained, facilitated, guided, informed, innovated, instructed, persuaded, set goals, simplified, stimulated, trained, taught.

Helping Skills: assessed, assisted, clarified, coached, counseled, delivered, demonstrated, diagnosed, educated, enabled, encouraged, exhibited, expedited, facilitated, familiarized, guided, motivated, referred, rehabilitated, represented.

Achievement Verbs: accomplished, attained, achieved, carried out, completed, consumated, expanded, finished, fulfilled, improved, obtained, pioneered, realized, reached, reduced (losses), resolved, restored, spearheaded, succeeded, transformed.

CASI step one:
List past achievements

Make a list of twenty things you have accomplished in your work, volunteer or personal life. Order is not important, but remember to use "action words", and to be specific.

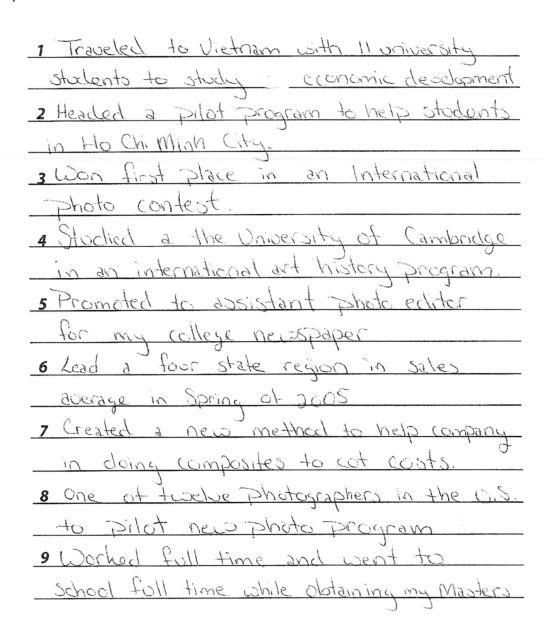

1. Traveled to Vietnam with 11 university students to study economic development
2. Headed a pilot program to help students in Ho Chi Minh City.
3. Won first place in an International photo contest.
4. Studied a the University of Cambridge in an international art history program.
5. Promoted to assistant photo editor for my college newspaper
6. Lead a four state region in sales average in Spring of 2005
7. Created a new method to help company in doing composites to cut costs.
8. One of twelve photographers in the U.S. to pilot new photo program
9. Worked full time and went to school full time while obtaining my Masters

10 Volunteered to help 6-7 homeless women with their career & education goals.

11 Successfully planned and executed a surprised anniversary party for my parents.

12 Created method at college paper to assist with the design to be more pleasing.

13 Received positive reviews from troubled school that no one else would go to.

14 Spent two weeks traveling around Switzerland, Italy and France.

15 Conducted a research project with 4 other students to study white poverty.

16 Been a vegetarian for the past seven years.

17 Developed a method to get young children to eat more fruits & veggies.

18 Supervised a staff of 15 college photographers

19 Wrote a grant to fund initiatives for a large city.

20 Won 3rd place in the State of Michigan College Photo Contest.

CASI step two:
Transfer the data to the CASI matrix

	1	2	3	4	5	6	7	8	9	10	11	12	13	14	15	16	17	18	19	20
accounting	X			X															X	
administered	X	X			X	X		X			X	X	X	X	X		X	X	X	X
advertised							X													
advised					X			X		X		X			X	X	X	X		
analyzed		X					X		X	X	X	X			X	X	X		X	
artistic			X	X	X	X		X				X	X	X			X	X	X	X
assembled	X	X	X			X		X	X	X	X		X	X	X			X		
audited																				
briefed							X	X				X			X					
budgeted	X			X					X		X		X						X	
conceptualized		X	X	X		X	X	X				X	X		X	X	X			X
construction trades																				
controlled the event		X			X						X		X		X		X	X		
coordinated	X			X	X	X		X	X	X	X	X	X	X	X		X	X	X	X
counseled individualsor groups										X										
created contracts																				
created ideas	X	X	X		X	X	X	X	X	X	X	X	X		X	X	X	X	X	X
customer relations						X	X	X					X							

	1	2	3	4	5	6	7	8	9	10	11	12	13	14	15	16	17	18	19	20
data processing															X					
designed		X	X		X	X	X	X	X		X	X	X		X	X	X	X	X	X
developed procedures/processes		X		X	X	X	X	X				X	X							
developed questions		X					X			X					X					
diagnosed																		X		
economized/saved												X	X							
edited			X		X			X				X						X	X	X
electrical																				
enforced rules/procedures							X					X						X		
established policy/procedures	X	X					X	X				X						X		
established systems		X				X		X	X	X	X	X		X		X				
evaluated	X		X	X			X	X				X							X	X
figured/calculated																				
financial planning/monitoring	X			X							X		X						X	
fixed something							X					X	X							
grant writing																			X	
initiated action	X	X								X				X		X				
instructed/trained					X							X				X		X		
interviewed		X																		
inventoried																				
led people					X					X	X							X		

	1	2	3	4	5	6	7	8	9	10	11	12	13	14	15	16	17	18	19	20
manged people/things	X				X			X	X	X	X							X		
marketing						X														
mechanical drawing																				
modified		X					X	X	X			X	X			X	X		X	
monitored					X			X	X	X	X				X		X	X		
motivated					X					X				X			X	X		
negotiated																				
observed	X	X			X		X			X					X	X	X	X		
operated	X	X				X		X	X				X			X				
organized people		X			X		X			X	X						X	X		
organized projects	X	X	-	X	X	X	X	X			X	X	X		X		X	X	X	X
perceived idea	X	X	X	X	X	X	X	X	X		X	X	X	X	X	X	X	X		X
persuaded																				
planned				X					X		X	X		X	X			X	X	
problem solving	X	X			X	X	X		X		X	X	X			X	X	X		
produced item			X																	
program development		X					X	X				X	X					X		
programmed computer																				
promoted					X															
promoted program								X												
public relations								X					X							

	1	2	3	4	5	6	7	8	9	10	11	12	13	14	15	16	17	18	19	20
purchased											X			X						
repair work																				
researched	X														X					
resolved problem		X			X		X	X		X	X	X	X			X	X		X	
scheduled				X							X				X			X		
seminar or workshop speaker							X													
sold/marketed																				
spoke in public					X		X													
supervised					X					X		X						X		
taught/lectured		X			X		X			X		X					X	X		
tended																				
time management	X			X	X			X	X		X				X	X		X		
troubleshooting		X			X		X		X		X	X	X				X	X		
wrote reports															X				X	
wrote/published					X															X

CASI step three:
Identify top factors

Now make two lists. The first is a list of your top ten hits. To do this, record the ten categories from the matrix that got the greatest number of marks. For the second list, record the five categories that are your favorites--things you really enjoy--even if they only got one mark. You'll use these combined fifteen factors to begin to describe your next career position.

Top ten hits:

1. Coordinated
2. Created Ideas
3. Designed
4. Organized Projects
5. Perceived Ideas
6. Problem Solving
7. Administered
8. Assembled
9. Resolved Problem
10. Established Systems

Five favorites:

1. Analyzed
2. Manage People / Things
3. Planned
4. Taught / Lectured
5. Troubleshooting

CASI step four:
Prioritize results

From the two lists on the preceeding page, list three to five career abilities that you are both capable of and willing to use.

1 Create Ideas

2 Organize Projects

3 Problem Solve

4 Analyze

5 Manage People/Things

CASI step five:
Develop narratives

Write a brief, three-sentence narrative for each career accomplishment listed above. Select the best example where that accomplishment was the essential element in making the event happen. First, state what you did, second, who you did it for, and third, describe the results.

Next, write a second three-sentence narrative for each career accomplishment. Select an example from another time (a three to five year spread is best) or place.

Finish by writing a third three-sentence accomplishment narrative for each of your accomplishments. This time pick a good example from a non-paying job or perhaps a voluntary contribution.

1.a I created new ways to utilize my photographers potential. I did it for CM Newspaper. This allowed the paper to be more pleasing to the readers eye and become award winning in photography

1.b

1.c

2.a I organized a promotional table for the Vietnames Tet Event. I did this for a graduate professor. The result was to draw more attention to our program and enroll 10 people for next years trip.

2.b

2.c

3.a I created a new method to complete composite forms. I did this for Lifeway Photography. The results was I taught this method to a group of 20.

3.b

3.c

4.a I analyed data for a program in Vietnam that allowed univesity student to work with city officials. I did this for my university. The result was we received the funding and the program was a go ahead.

4.b

4.c

5.a One of twelve photographers in the U.S. picked to manage a new project. I did this for Lifeway Photography. The result was I increased sales by half and was one of the leaders in sale average in the country.

5.b

5.c

Assessment: assignment four

Analyze the data

What knowledge, skills and abilities
do you want to use in the next phase of your career?

I want a career where I can
solve problems, create new ideas,
analyze data and manage people and
projects.

What successes have you had in using
this set of knowledge, skills and abilities?

I have success in these areas from
previous job experiences and through
my education.

In the job market, where might this set of
knowledge, skills and abilities be valued?

These skills will valued in a career
when developing and problem solving
are key.

Research: assignment one

Exploring the O*net

1. Log on to the O*NET website (www.online.onetcenter.org).
2. Click on the "Find Occupations" tab on the left hand side.
3. Enter key words from your CAREER ACCOMPLISHMENTS list.
4. List below the occupations that you want to research further.

Job title _Urban and Regional Planner_
Median Income _$56,630_
Specific needs or training _4 year degree, experience_
Projected Growth _Faster than average (14% to 20%)_

Job title _Social & Community Services Manager_
Median Income _$52,070_
Specific needs or training _4 year degree, on the job training_
Projected Growth _Much Faster than average (21% or higher)_

Job title _City & Regional Planning Aides_
Median Income _$33,760_
Specific needs or training _1 to 2 years of experience & training_
Projected Growth _Average (7% to 13%)_

Job title _____
Median Income _____
Specific needs or training _____
Projected Growth _____

Job title _____
Median Income _____
Specific needs or training _____
Projected Growth _____

Job title _____
Median Income _____
Specific needs or training _____
Projected Growth _____

Exploring the Occupational Outlook Handbook

1. Log on to the OOH website (www. bls.gov/oco).
2. Search based on the data from your career accomplishments list.
3. Compare with the information from from the O*Net site.

Job title _Urban & Regional Planners_
Median Income _$56,630_
Specific needs or training _Most require a Master's degree_
Projected Growth _Increase 15% between 2006-2016_

Job title _Social Scientist_
Median Income _$43,731_
Specific needs or training _Master's degree or Ph.D_
Projected Growth _Increase 6% between 2006-2016_

Job title _Community Association Managers_
Median Income _$43,070_
Specific needs or training _Bachelor's or Master's degree_
Projected Growth _Increase 15% between 2006-2016_

Job title _____
Median Income _____
Specific needs or training _____
Projected Growth _____

Job title _____
Median Income _____
Specific needs or training _____
Projected Growth _____

Job title _____
Median Income _____
Specific needs or training _____
Projected Growth _____

Research: assignment two

Contacts lists

Based on your research in assignment one, select two or three career positions you would like to research further. Then list people you know in these fields who might give you an informational interview, or who can refer you to someone in the target field. Include contact information.

target position	who I know	who they know
Housing and Community Development Specialist	Ken Barker	Suzy White
Community Service Manager	Karen Suite	Lisa Black

Keeping track

Keep a record of who you have contacted, the date you met with them, the outcome of the meeting, and any follow-up activities, including a letter of thanks for their time.

person	date	outcome	follow-up	thanks
Ken Barker	7/28	Suzy White's contact info.	keep him updated	thank you note

Research: assignment three

Networking groups

Find out what sort of professional and social groups the members of your target position belong to by doing an online search. Make a note of upcoming meetings and prepare to attend them.

position	professional or social groups	meetings
Director of Community Development	Business and Professional Women	every other Monday
Social & Community Services Manager	Young Women Social Entrepreneurs	first Tuesday of every month

Research: assignment four

Developing your image

Consider the various aspects of the impression you make on potential employers through such things as the way you dress, your online and telephone presence. Keep track of these and other areas that could use improvement and what you are doing to develop them.

aspect	status	completed
wardrobe		X
professional email		X
business cards	Ordered and on their way	
voicemail		X
ringtone		X
MySpace	needs to be updated	
LinkedIn	needs to be updated	
personal website	don't have one	
Google presence	need to blog more	
LinkedIn		
other		

Research: assignment six

Describe your career position

You will now describe your next career position in a number of different ways to develop your objective.

Write a ten-word description of your perfect job (this need not be a job title).

I create neighborhoods and communities for low income families

How would you describe this job simply, to your grandmother, for example?

I redevelop neighborhoods

How would you describe this position to a professional in that field?

I create vibrant neighborhoods that include economic prosperity and affordable housing for low income families.

Now give as inclusive a description of this position as possible. Include salary, benefits, travel opportunites and obligations, insurance, and any other considerations that are imprtant to you.

I want to work for a government agency making at least $45,000 starting off. I would like to have insurance and enough vacation time so I can travel home at least 1-2 a year.

What examples will you use to show that you can do this job?

Since I don't have as much work experience in this field. I would use examples from my volunteer work and project I did during my graduate degree.

Marketing materials: assignment one

Develop a clear objective statement for your resume

A good objective statement should be written to encourage the reader to read the rest of your resume. Use the following formula to help you write your own.

Step 1) Begin with the level of responsibility you want. . .
"A leadership position…"
"A supervisory position…"
"Management position…"

Alternate Step 1) You may want to begin with the position title you want…
"A sales position…"
"A financial consultant position…"
"Project Manager…"

Step 2) Follow with the industry that suits you most . . .
"…in a manufacturing firm…"
"…for an international logistics company…"
"…in healthcare…"

Step 3) Insert a connecting "flex" word . . .
"encompassing" (for executive)
"utilizing" (for "hands-on" position)
"involving" (for mid-level)

Step 4) Put in two or three key skills (as defined in CASI)
"no more than 3 -- it dilutes your power"
"use skills that MOST describe…"
"use wording from O*NET"

Step 5) You may want to add geographic preference (if it is important)
"…in an international firm…"
"…in Portland, Oregon…"

continued next page

Step 6) You may want to add something about the company
…a closely held firm…"
…a Fortune 500 company…"

Step 7) Finish with something you can DO FOR the company
"…to increase international sales."
"…to reduce environmental waste, thereby increasing profitability."

Examples

"A management position within a small, family manufacturing business that will utilize my proven ability to reduce waste and increase corporate profitability."

"Sales management position in a major international firm that involves my abilities to develop, motivate and lead teams to successfully accomplish difficult goals and objectives."

"A senior level finance manager position in a Oregon-based company requiring flexible management skills, creative problem solving and effective communication, oriented towards deadlines while maximizing the corporate bottom line."

Write your own objective statement.

A leadership position in community development that utilizes my problem solving, analytical and managing skills to create healty neighborhoods.

Marketing materials: assignment two

Use this chart to keep track of your marketing materials.

type	draft	completed	updated
chronological resume		X	
functional resume	X		
hybrid resume	X		
e-resume	X		
email resume (pdf)		X	
Monster profile		X	
Jobdango profile		X	
MySpace profile	X		
LinkedIn profile	X		
website			
CV			
portfolio			
brag book			
capabilities statement			
10-word overview	X		
elevator pitch	X		
60 second pitch			
90 second pitch			
networking pitch			
social pitch			

Marketing materials: assignment three

Define your Unique Selling Proposition

A USP is a concise statement of what sets you apart from everyone else who does the job you do.

To begin, review your key accomplishments from the CASI exercises. Also, think about the language people you have met in informal interviews and the language they use to describe their needs. Consider the examples given here, and see how they not only say what the person does, but what's special about the way they do it. There are more tips on refining your USP in chapter 4, Strategy, on page 75.

"I specialize in working with thirty-nine year old women who want to run a marathon on their fortieth birthday."
Chiropractor

"I recruit, train and motivate people to reach their highest potential."
Found work as a Corporate Trainer.

"My expertise is the intersection of science, business and regulatory issues."
Found work doing business development for an environmental cience company.

"I love to work with difficult people."
Project Manager

Write your Unique Selling Proposition.

I visualize vibrant neighborhoods that portray economic prosperity & affordable housing for low income families.

Strategy: assignment one

Setting targets, goals and objectives

To do this, you'll need some Post-it notes and a wall.

On one of the Post-it notes , write down your target, for example, a career position you wan to attain.

Post it in the center of the wall.

Now, brainsorm to come up with all of the things you will need to do in order to achieve your target. Include people you will have to meet, posting your resume online, get some dress socks...any aspect of the ARMS process you've learned throughout this book, as well as anything else that comes to mind that is related to achieving your target. Don't "self-edit" at this point. Just make notes of things to do.

You now have a Post-it with a target on a wall, and a bunch of activities related to that target.

Now, around that target, put the notes that you've come up with into related groups. For example, update your resume and post resume online would be posted close to one another. Buy dress socks and make a trip to the dry cleaners would go together. Each group is a goal, such as "resume" or "personal presentation".

Finally, re-order the notes according to priority. What is most important? What has to happen first? Clearly, you will want to update your resume before posting it online, so it should be on top of that group. Each of the things you must do are objectives to achieving your goals.

Once you've done this with all of your notes, transfer the information to a piece of paper. At the top write down your target, and below that record all the the goals and objectives in the order you must follow to achieve them. You can take these objectives and use the folowing exercise to moniter your progress in achieving them.

What is your target?

To create healthy neighborhoods.

List your goals for achieving that target.

Goal number one:

Finish Strategic Plan

Goal number two:

Develop Marketing Materials

Goal number three:

Make a name for myself

Goal number four:

Prepare for Interviews

Goal number five:

Goal number one: Finish Strategic Plan

To be completed by (date): 8/10

Goal details: To finish materials that support my Strategic Plan.

Objectives: (1) Meet about 360 assessment
(2) Identify benchmarks
(3) Schedule & Prioritize

Benchmarks: (1) 360 done by 8/8
(2) benchmarks 8/9
(3) Schedule & Prioritize 8/10

Results: I will have a plan follow

Follow-up activities:

Goal number two: Develop marketing Materials

To be completed by (date): 8/18

Goal details: Finish & Update materials used to market myself.

Objectives: (1) Update Resume
(2) Create Business Cards
(3) Create Coverletters
(4) Create a Blog
(5) Update LinkedIn, Myspace & Facebook profiles

Benchmarks: (1) Resume by 8/10 have 5 people look at it.
(2) Create business cards by 8/5
(3) Create coverletters & have 5 people proof them by 8/10
(4) Create a blog by 8/15 & blog once a week
(5) Update profiles by 8/18

Results: Materials will be update & prepared for interviews & networking.

Follow-up activities: Once a month double Check everything to make sure it is current.

Goal number three: Make a Name for Myself

To be completed by (date): 9/4

Goal details: When people think of community development they think of Christina.

Objectives: (1) Join a professional/networking group
(2) Interview 10 people in the comm. dev. field.
(3) Find an organization to volunteer with.
(4) Find a mentor

Benchmarks: (1) Join at least 2 groups by 9/4
(2) Interview at least 2 people per week
(3) Find an org. by 9/1
(4) Find a mentor by 9/4

Results: Get my name out there and start meeting people in this field.

Follow-up activities: To continue interviewing until I find my career.

Goal number four: Prepare for Interviews

To be completed by (date): 8/25

Goal details: Develop materials to prepare myself for interviews

Objectives: (1) develop questions
(2) Practice answers + achievement stories
(3) Do mock Interviews

Benchmarks: (1) develop 15 questions for interviews
(2) Have my answers & achievements set and practiced by 8/25
(3) Do one mock interview per week.

Results: To ensure interviews go more smoothly.

Follow-up activities: To change questions & answers accordingly

Strategy: assignment two

Prioritizing your opportunities.

Evaluate and prioritize activities and opportunities or introductions according to your objectives. Each activity, opportunity, or introduction will be sorted into one of three "buckets", labeled as high priority, medium priority, or low priority.
Into the high priority bucket, note opportunities that directly related to your goals, and that you are prepared to follow through on. You should act on priority bucket opportunities within the next twenty-four hours. In the medium priority bucket, put opportunities that are in some way related to your goals, and act on them sometime in the coming week. In the low priority bucket, put opportunities that seem unrelated or that you don't expect much out of. Follow up on these only once you've attended to the high and medium priority buckets. Be aware, however, that an opportunity can move from one bucket to another, based on new information, or your own personal preparedness.

Consider some examples. You want to work in the footwear industry. Someone you know has lunch on Tuesdays with the president of Nike, and has offered to introduce you. Sounds like a "high priority bucket" opportunity, doesn't it? Not if you haven't researched the company, or if you don't have a decent shirt to wear. Now your priorities become research and wardrobe, so you will be prepared to pursue this opportunity.

Or perhaps a friend of yours knows about your career goals and tells you to call his cousin, who is "really into shoes". Doesn't sound like much. But it turns out that this cousin who is "really into shoes" designs them for Gucci. What seemed a low priority item has now become high priority.

Keep track of your opportunites and the contact information for both the person who referred you and the opportunity itself. Under plan of action, include time and date information. Be sure and thank people who open doors for you.

High priority bucket

opportunity	contact info	plan of action	thanks
Schedule meeting w/ org to volunteer with.	Call Sarah back 555-8073	Start volunteering by next week.	

Medium priority bucket

opportunity	contact info	plan of action	thanks
Attend a women's prof. meeting this week	Meeting at 1223 SE main St.	have material ready & rehearsed by meeting.	

Low priority bucket

opportunity	contact info	plan of action	thanks
Call Aunt Marie's friend who does "housing".	Tom 555-6304	Once my marketing materials are finish, call.	

LaVergne, TN USA
24 March 2011
221365LV00001B/26/P